MW01181195

BLESSINGS
BY THE
DOZEN

AN AUTOBIOGRAPHY WITH PERSONAL TESTIMONIES

PAUL KEE-HUA HANG, JR.

Outskirts Press, Inc.
Denver, Colorado

Blessings by the Dozen
An Autobiography with Personal Testimonies
All Rights Reserved
Copyright © 2006 Paul Kee-Hua Hang, Jr.

Outskirts Press
http://www.outskirtspress.com

ISBN-10: 1-59800-431-X
ISBN-13: 978-1-59800-431-1

Outskirts Press and the "OP" logo are trademarks belonging to Outskirts Press, Inc.

Printed in the United States of America

CONTENTS

PREFACE
WE WILL GLORIFY THE LORD!

This book is written in an attempt to document all of the significant events in the life of an Asian Singaporean whose life's experiences are truly both unique as well as one of bitter sweet struggles and blessings. In non-fiction fashion, this book describes the life of a Chinese Singaporean who was born into a world of poverty and great depression in the early 1930's and who had lived through the difficult days of the World War II years of 1940-1944. This is a story of my life's journey through some 70 years' of great blessings and excitement, of wonderfully miraculous events and painful struggles.

From initial concept to putting my thoughts in writing, in my quiet time of reflection, I am ever so deeply mindful of God's divine touch upon my life and of how God has somehow shaped my life and ordained my destiny. In true Christian perspective and understanding, I have tried to describe all of the major events in my life and in so doing, God has revealed His sovereign purpose and direction for my life and that of my family. Truly, all the members of my large "Hang" family of Singapore have been greatly blessed by the Lord.

Coming from very poor and humble beginnings, I was born to Chinese immigrant parents, the Rev. and Mrs. Paul Sing-Hoh Hang, in the midst of the worldwide depression on April 3, 1932. As early Chinese immigrants from the Fukien Province (southern China), my parents were called to full-time Christian ministry to the Island Republic (a former British colony) of Singapore in the early 1920's. As a young teenager, I received my early education in the Anglo-Chinese Methodist School in Singapore before receiving my higher college education in the U.S.A., thus resulting in half of my 73 years living in Singapore and the rest in the U.S.A., initially as a "foreign student" and eventually as a U.S. citizen together with my wife and our four children.

Growing up as a "P.K." (preacher's kid), I was one of 12 siblings (at times I was nicknamed one of the "even dozen" kids) consisting of six boys and six girls. In the old days, it seemed like the Chinese tradition of having many children perhaps it was the common practice, and was considered an asset especially where many helping hands were needed in the traditionally farming communities in China. In the case of our family, the helping hands of the older siblings came in handy for the many household chores, including the caring and mentoring of the younger siblings.

Life in our early childhood and teenage years (especially in a large family with many siblings) was truly challenging and not a bed of roses by any means. As an example, even the basic necessities of life were found lacking, such necessities as adequate nutritional food, clothing, sanitation and educational needs. This was mainly because of our large family with as many as 14 mouths to feed, and living on my father's meager "shoe-string" family budget. By modern day standards, we would be deemed to be living in deprivation. We were instilled with the idea that no edible food should ever be wasted and that throwing away any food was to be frowned upon. Thus the older siblings were especially instilled with a greater sense of value for many things especially food.

For me, what seemed most challenging were the demands of my family obligations and parental obedience that were the hallmarks of the Chinese traditional values, perhaps more pronounced in my family situation and circumstances. Strict moral ethics and disciplines dictated father's high standards of behavior and self-discipline. As the sole bread winner and head of his family, my father was somewhat of an authoritarian in that all of his family lived by his very strict rules of filial piety, discipline and obedience As an example, no one was allowed to leave home without a valid reason or without my father's express permission. In other words, we were mostly homebound, with few exceptions in our teenage and adolescent years.

We lived most of our early childhood and teenage years in a church environment where my father devoted all of his life to serving God, building up the Hinghwa Methodist Church, Singapore and to "extending the kingdom of God". His lifelong desire was to "Go ye, therefore and teach all nations, baptizing them in the name of the Father and of the Son and of the Holy Ghost" (quoting Matt. 28:19). Along with my father's life mission and vocation, our large family of 12 siblings lived in a 3-room church parsonage directly above the old church located at No. 27 Sam Leong Road. My father was also the caretaker and "unpaid" janitor. He had assumed the all-encompassing responsibilities as the pastor, preacher, shepherd of his "flock" and the caretaker, so it was expected of his children to assist him in the maintenance and upkeep of the church premises. As disciplined and obedient children, we had to emulate my father in his high standard of cleanliness and orderliness. Those early childhood and teenage years were indeed challenging years for me!

In addition to some accounts of my childhood and my experiences living in Singapore, this book will shed some light on my parents' family and grandparents in China. They had left their homeland China in response to God's call to ministry and to serve their fellow Chinese immigrants in the far-away foreign country. I wanted to capture some aspects of their lives as God's servants so as to perpetuate their memory and as a legacy to the future Hang generations. My parents truly deserve much praise and credit in raising and upbringing their 12 children through the difficult pre-war and World War II years and surviving the hardships of a major world war!

In the following pages, I have attempted to describe some of the significant events and circumstances of my life, including those of my own immediate family, as youngsters growing up in the Island Republic of Singapore and also as new immigrants to the United States of America. Our newly found life and experiences in the United States also testify to our faith in a gracious and loving Heavenly Father and His promise that, "All things work together for good to those that love God" (quoting Romans 8:28). I have also attempted to portray some aspects of the lives of my four brothers – Peter, John, David and Benjamin, whose lives were tragically cut short by cancer. Our family was grieved to lose our dear sister Rebecca who was called home to be with the Lord after a short illness in 1999. In the later chapters of this book, I was inspired to write those testimonies of the miraculous events in my life and to *"Glorify the Lord!"* The final chapter of this book describes my first ever trip to China in December of 2000 as well as my first impressions of our motherland China that I was privileged to visit.

FOREWORD

This book is appropriately entitled "Blessings by the Dozen" as indeed it is written to glorify God and to capture the precious memories in the lives of my twelve "Even Dozen" Hang siblings, my own family's life journey and lives of my brothers' and sisters' families, their achievements and successes. Truly, all of our lives have been greatly blessed beyond all expectations! Hence I am inspired to entitle this book "Blessings by the Dozen!"

As I reflect upon the many challenges and blessings we have all experienced through our difficult childhood and young adult years, it seems evident that God has turned all of our struggles and trials into great blessings as it is evident in the later years of our lives. All of us 6 boys and 6 girls, at times nicknamed, "the Even Dozen Kids" have been so blessed by God such that we should truly thank God and Glorify Him! In reflecting upon the lives of my siblings, it is also appropriate to reflect upon the many blessings that God has bestowed upon our respective families and children - even upon the younger 2nd and 3rd generations. The history of the Hang family that began with the departure of our parents from China does not seem enviable in view of the dispersion of the family members around the world and living our separate lives.

I have painstakingly put to writing all of the significant events in the lives of my parents as well as the next generation. While the undertaking has significance to the younger generation, it is the recollection of facts relating to our lives' journey of spiritual warfare, personal sacrifice and dedication to family and the Church, bonded together by our deep love of God that will speak volumes to our families and friends. My father, the late Rev. Paul S.H. Hang Sr. was a strong-willed man who was not afraid to brave the hardships to pursue his conviction and devotion to serving God and to preach the gospel to all the nations. The strength of his conviction and dedication caused him to faithfully serve God with little regard for the consequences and sacrifice of his own comfort and well-being, whether it is about material wealth or otherwise. He was a man of great intellect and a highly accomplished scholar whose only desire was to honor God's call to ministry and to shepherd His flock. We count him among the few true models of complete dedication to Christ and His Church in the present generation.

With God and the church dominating his world, my father did not have the luxury of spending quality time with his wife and children, but his love for us was deep and beyond question. Even though traditional Chinese fathers rarely openly expressed their love and affection, we have fond memories of my dear father and his love for us. It was my father's strong desire and demand that his children spend much time together in the church that added to our sense of oneness. He had spent many years of toil and laboring to build the Hinghwa Methodist Church. In the early years of the church, my father and his fellow workers faced many trials and challenges in very difficult economic times and circumstances. But the church flourished in spite of the great hardships as my father persevered in his labor of love for the Lord. He was greatly thrilled to see the fruits of his labors as the Hinghwa Methodist Church in Singapore grew and matured over the many years! The growth of my father's church in Singapore has been unprecedented over the years, soon it will be celebrating its 100th Anniversary in a few years' time.

DEDICATION

This book is dedicated to:

1. The Glory of God and for His everlasting love, mercy and grace;
2. My loving wife and children, namely Doris Hang, Deborah Harms, Phoebe Fung, Dr. Timothy Hang, and Dr. Muriel Burk who have given me great joy and great meaning to my purpose-driven life;
3. My beloved parents, the late Rev. & Mrs. Paul S. H. Hang Sr., who devoted their lives to serving God and to extending the kingdom of God, raising and nurturing their twelve "cheaper by the dozen" children;
4. My "Hang" siblings who have greatly influenced my life in one way or another;
5. The memory of my dear friends in Christ, Mr. & Mrs. J. E. Love without whose financial support I would not have been able to receive my college education in America.

CHAPTER 1
FAMILY ROOTS

The "Hang" family roots date back to the olden days of Chinese traditions and culture in mainland China, specifically to my parent's home village of Sienyu in Fukien Province, South China. It is where many of their relatives and next of kin still live today. In the midst of the endless rows of rice fields was where mother's huge "Ng" family mansion stood, with its classical oriental roof, spacious rooms and hallways. It looked like an old native longhouse. Its unique architecture included a spacious cement courtyard at the front where many children played amidst farm animals such as chicken, ducks, pigs, and dogs and cats.

This was the scene that greeted me when I first visited my mother's old family home in 2000. As I walked on the 500 feet dirt road and over a shaky wooden bridge towards the stately mansion, I was greeted by at least 40 people seemingly coming out from everywhere! They were later introduced to me as my mother's many relatives and next of kin, as well as distant relatives, all of whom lived in the family mansion as well as around the family compound.

I learned that a good number of my mother's family lived and worked on the family farm in Nam May. There was plenty of work for everyone on the huge rice fields and vegetable farms for those who chose to make a living on the family farm. Some of the more enterprising younger members were able to earn better wages outside the family farmland. In doing so, they had the financial means to build more modern brick houses on the family land adjacent to the old family mansion. A few of my mother's nephews were even so enterprising as to start an industry raising huge quantities of eels in large aquariums. They were exporting them overseas, as well as to the Japanese market. It turned out to be a lucrative business until the devaluation of the Japanese yen that made the business unprofitable and it slowed down considerably.

That was my first visit ever to my parents' homeland and the well-known "Ng" family mansion that we had heard much about over the years but had never been able to see it in person. In fact, until then, I had never seen any part of China. Having not known any of my relatives in China, my sister, Ruth, who was traveling with me, and I were somewhat lost in the midst of about 40 relatives whose names we did not know! We were welcomed with a sumptuous luncheon consisting of approximately 12 delicious dishes of noodles and seafood entrees. After the luncheon, I was amazed to see the men offering cigarettes to one another for dessert. Cigarette was not my "cup of tea" so I settled, instead, for a cup of Chinese tea.

As I was given a tour of the mansion, my mother's nephew cautioned me to watch where I was going. There was very little lighting in the house and there were potholes everywhere on the earthen floors. There were also many old, unwanted pieces of furniture, earthenware, and rubbish scattered all over the house. As we walked through the many dark and dingy rooms and hallways, I was shown a dark and dingy back room, which my mother's nephew mentioned used to be my mother's bedroom before she was married and left for Singapore. Being the eldest of the girls, my mother supposedly had the best room in the mansion. As I toured the mansion and visited with mother's nephews and their family, my thoughts traveled back about 80 years to the time when my father and my mother had met.

My father was born in 1901, into a poor family in the remote village of Sai Yong in Fukien. He met my mother at the Seven Steps Church in Sienyu City. My mother, who was also born in 1901, came from a relatively well-to-do peasant family. They both had the desire to serve God; he felt called to preach the gospel, and she wanted to enter a Woman's Bible College. Little did she know that she would one day become a preacher's wife and prayer partner instead, and serve in the women's ministry at the church alongside her husband.

Father had graduated from the Nanking Theological Seminary and had returned to Sienyu to meet his wife-to-be and family. According to mother, wedding plans were discussed between my father's family in Sai Yong (some 20 miles away) and the "Ng" family in Sienyu. While my mother came from a family of a wealthy landowner, my father's family was very poor. Because of that, mother's family did not favor father initially, as he was the only son of a poor peasant family and whose father was jobless. Seeing that my father had professed to become a preacher of the gospel, the well-to-do Ng family preferred to see my mother betrothed to a wealthier gentleman and not a poor village preacher!

Little is known of my father's siblings or relatives, other than the only son of a younger sister (now deceased), who now lives in Sienyu with his family, having moved away from his hometown village of Sai Yong. According to my father, his father was not a good provider for his family and his hard-working mother supported the family as a "bible-reader", in addition to caring for her family's needs. His mother earned her reputation as a "bible-reader" by going to the homes of various folks who had little or no education and were unable to read the Bible. There, she would read the Bible to them in the Hinghwa (Chinese) dialect.

I have met my paternal grandfather only once, when my father paid his way from China to visit Singapore. According to my father, my grandfather had the opportunity to work in the tin mines of Malaysia, but he did not make good of that opportunity and eventually returned back to China, jobless. My grandfather's addiction to opium not only caused great misery to the family, he led a meaningless life and eventually died of poor health at a young age.

My parents eventually married and I imagined it had to be a beautiful wedding celebration in the local church in Sienyu called the Seven Steps Church where they had met and fallen in love, and the reception at the old mansion must have been very grand. My parents had an old studio portrait of the bride and groom, both resplendent in their hand-quilted wedding attire and father wearing what appeared to be a quilted skirt! Other than that, I knew very little else of their wedding or honeymoon which took place in 1926.

According to my mother, back in those days, they traveled from one village to another by means of a wooden carriage carried on a wooden pole by two strong and able men. Traveling from Sienyu to Amoy took several days, going through the back roads, and there was always the danger of robbers. That was how my father traveled from Nanking to Sienyu to visit mother, as well as when he and his newly-married wife left Sienyu and traveled to Amoy, which was along the coast, to board a steamship for the faraway land of Singapore. As I cruised in a minibus on a modern toll road in December 2000, memories of my mother's such stories came to mind as I traveled from Amoy to Sienyu and back to Amoy again. That was also the same route that many early Chinese immigrants traveled from mainland China to Singapore, Malaysia and other parts of South East Asia. Seemingly, my parents were the early pioneers in the migration of thousands of Chinese from their motherland. My parents not only had to face the challenge of church planting and raising a family in a strange new land, they also found themselves becoming guardians and mentors to many friends and relatives from their home village in China.

During the many years while living in Singapore, my father never could find the right opportunity to visit his homeland (except once in 1928), besides it was not safe for him to return, for fear of being kidnapped. On the other hand, my mother, together with my eldest sister, Mary, had the opportunity to visit her family and relatives in Sienyu once. In 1947, for the first time since leaving home, my mother had the opportunity to visit her homeland, sailing by ship from Singapore to Amoy, and then traveling the difficult back roads. Other than that, they would only communicate with their loved ones in China via letters and sending money to help with their relatively poor and needy family and next of kin in mainland China.

Our "Hang" family name, when literally translated from the written Chinese language, had an uncomplimentary meaning in the English language. It should have been correctly spelled "Fan", as in the spoken Mandarin. Though insignificant as it may seem to some people, the incorrect spelling of the "Hang" family name has often caused us some embarrassment. This was because of my father's strong desire to adhere to the spoken Hinghwa dialect of his small village of Sai Yong. Unlike my mother's hometown village of Sienyu (now Sienyu City), Sai Yong appeared rather backward, with little development of the infrastructure. Sienyu City was a flourishing fishing village, where the infrastructure showed more industrial growth. It had a number of retail shops as well as many churches in the city and suburbs.

Such was the beginning of my parents' lives' journey from their homeland to the land of Singapore, where they lived for over 40 years. They devoted their lives completely to the ministry of reaching out to the lost and to spreading the gospel of Jesus Christ in Singapore. They lived a life of great struggles and hardship as they raised a large family of 12 children. Their sacrifices, in turn, brought many blessings to the next generations living in Singapore and as well as overseas, including the United States of America.

"HANG" FAMILY ROOTS

Our Parents – God's Servants
Taken soon after Father's retirement - 1969

Family picture (minus Ruth) – 1950

Celebrating our parents' 25th Silver Wedding Anniversary

The old Hinghwa Methodist Church At No. 27 Sam Leong Road – 1930's

Father proudly shows off his new Hinghwa Methodist Church at No. 93, Kitchener Road

Visiting General Conference with brother Benjamin in Indianapolis – 1980

Esther visits Paul in Roselle – 1996

Our first "Hang" Siblings Reunion – Alaskan Cruise – 1991

Mother with girls (left to right) Sarah, Esther, Ruth and Elizabeth

Bidding "good bye" as Mary left for U.K.
(left to right: Paul Jr. Mary, Rebecca, Peter)

CHAPTER 2
OUR PARENTS – GOD'S SERVANTS

I have fond memories of our parents – their lives in China and their God-ordained ministry in Singapore that had deeply impacted many including my twelve siblings.

When my father was young, he had met a number of early American missionaries serving in China. A missionary by the name of Rev. William Hollister who had met my father, remarked, "He is a smart and promising young man of God. I will help him through his high school and send him to the Nanking Theological Seminary for training in preparation for God's work".

With that, my father's ministry was birthed and as a result, impacted many lives in Singapore. After they were married, and with the blessing of my father's missionary mentor and their God-fearing parents, my parents left everything in China for a faraway country called Singapore, in answer to a call to "preach the gospel". He seemed the ideal choice for the Hinghwa Methodist Church, which he ended up serving for over 40 years!

According to my father, "In the early 1920's when the Hinghwa-speaking congregation in Singapore badly needed a qualified pastor, none was found who could speak the unique "dialect". So the church elders sent a letter to Nanking asking for the young preacher, Hang Hoh-Kee, a.k.a. Hang Sing-Hoh, who was my father, to come to Singapore to fill the vacant post as quickly as possible. Never did my father imagine that he would serve in this same church for 40 long and fruitful years!

In his voluminous book, "My Christian Testimony" (1970 edition), my father painstakingly wrote in great detail about the historic events of the Hinghwa Methodist Church in Singapore. This book was his pride and joy! The present-day Hinghwa Methodist Church bears witness to the fruits of his labor and his wholehearted dedication to build the church and to extend God's kingdom on earth. In his book are many stories of the early church, as well as his Christian testimonies and sermons. He also wrote inspiring stories of the hardships and struggles of the early church in Singapore, and of the difficulties and challenges of reaching out to the local community. My father's autobiography documented everything from the history of the early Hinghwa Methodist Church from its roots in mainland China, the work of the early missionaries to China, to his ministry in Singapore. He also wrote about the church's history, major evangelistic events in Singapore and Malaysia, and his own family.

When the Hinghwa Methodist Church was built at 93 Kitchener Road in 1950, it was his dream come true and he prophesied that it would grow by leaps and bounds! After the sale of the old "shop house" church at No. 27 Sam Leong Road, plans were drawn up for the new church building at No. 93 Kitchener Road. My father insisted that extra foundation material be provided because he envisioned that the Hinghwa Methodist Church would see unprecedented spiritual and physical growth beyond anyone's imagination. He wanted extra "bakau" (wooden) piles for the building foundation as he believed that the church would grow much bigger and taller and that it would eventually rise several levels higher than what was planned.

Second to my parent's greatest achievement of "extending God's kingdom here on earth" was their "Cheaper by the Dozen" family. They had their first daughter in 1927, which was quickly followed by six boys and five girls about one child every year! My mother would have had 14 children had one not been lost through a miscarriage, and another daughter named "Boh Hua" who died at the very young age of 3 after a serious illness. They had struggled to build up the Hinghwa Methodist Church while providing for their 12 growing children during those difficult pre-World War II years.

It was because of God's provision that all of their twelve children were nurtured and well cared for throughout the early depression of the 1930s, and the World War II years of 1940-1944. It was a real challenge for them to raise twelve children on my father's small salary and we were very needy. We lived in very tight quarters in the church parsonage above the church sanctuary at No.27 Sam Leong Road, which had only 3 bedrooms to accommodate the whole family of 14 souls. When the church moved to its new location at No. 93 Kitchener Road, the parsonage also had 3 small bedrooms with only one bathroom and one shower!

Somehow we managed to survive and overcame whatever obstacles came our way. As their children reached school age, my parents prayed for God to miraculously provide for their education – even to go to college. Their prayers were answered when doors were opened for six of their twelve children to go to America for their college education. We were also blessed with good career opportunities and a promising future with our own families. Hence, the "cheaper by the dozen" "Hang" children more than doubled in size over the years, bringing about a whole new younger generation!

In retrospect, I believe that it was my parents' moral strength of character and faith in God that sustained them through the years. It was their will to live purposefully and their strength of character that earned them a "well done, good and faithful servant" entry to heaven. They also possessed their deep love for Christ and His Church as seen in the tremendous growth and on-going ministry of the Hinghwa Methodist Church in Singapore.

CHAPTER 3
OUR "EVEN DOZEN" SIBLINGS

For the twelve brothers and sisters of our Hang family, living together as one big family was truly a unique experience of a lifetime! For us, the many challenges and difficulties were truly beyond our wildest expectations!

"Cheaper by the Dozen" is the title of an old family movie that is known to many. It was also the nickname given to our Hang family of twelve children growing up in an Oriental setting and surrounded by the traditions and culture in the old colonial environment of the old country of Singapore – now known as the independent Republic of Singapore – a small British trading post of the 19th century.

We were a unique bunch of twelve children growing up in a poverty-stricken Chinese preacher's church home. As children, we experienced many frightening and fascinating episodes. We were living with our Chinese-educated parents who taught us to speak the Hinghwa-speaking Chinese dialect. Although we were going to the mission-sponsored English schools, English was not easily spoken in our family conversations. It was naturally more convenient to speak our mother tongue Chinese.

Imagine our plight and predicament when we were confronted by those so-called "red-haired" (literally translated from the Chinese language for the word "European") missionary friends who often visited our home. On occasions when our parents invited these early missionary friends to dinner at our home, all of us were so nervous as to say "Look out! Our white missionary friends are coming! They are here and coming into our house!" We were not so much as afraid by our European friends, as we were of engaging in intelligent English conversation with them! We struggled to overcome this fear of speaking English that was taught to us in our schools! When our guests talked to us, we became tongue tight for lack of the proper English words to express ourselves, also because we were accustomed to speak our own dialect at home.

As much as father was always thrilled to invite his missionary friends for dinner at our home, my mother and the older girls had to work extra hard in the kitchen. Mother became well-known among our missionary friends for her delicious Chinese fried vermicelli noodles and her one of a kind delicious sour-tasting beef soup – a favorite of our many family friends. As little children, we were too nervous as to be visible or to come out of the "wood work", so to speak, to meet our 'foreign' guests.

Our old missionary friends said, "Well, well, come all you wonderful children!. Let us see how well you all look – all the twelve of you little 'rascals', one, two, three, four, five, six, seven, eight, nine, ten, eleven and twelve! Twelve? Really? Or shall we call you "Cheaper by the Dozen!" "Hang" children. What a remarkable bunch of children – an even dozen of twelve (6 boys and 6 girls) altogether! How nice and how marvelous! That reminds us of the favorite American movie by that title! Rev. Hang, what a job it must have been to raise these many children?" As father and mother spoke very little English, their dinner conversation was mostly about the children and delicious food.

Then there was the problem of feeding and raising all the twelve of us. Most of the time, the older siblings would have to eat first in order to be freed to spoon feed the younger kids. This practice seemed to work well to help mother out with her many chores but often some younger kids would grumble saying, "It is not fair! There is not much left of our favorite food for us little ones! The older ones had eaten all the good food!" Then Mom or Dad would say, "Now, now, you little ones behave yourselves! Don't you think that Mom would have saved up some of the good food for you? Besides, don't you think that the older ones deserve a little better food for all of their hard work to help out with Mom's many household chores?" Silence then prevailed!

In reality, there were many problems and obstacles facing our parents and our kids. But somehow everyone had learnt to overcome the difficulties and managed to cope with every situation – from lack of plentiful food and toys to hand me down clothing, shoes, beds to sleep on, school books, desks for study space, bookshelves and a whole host of daily needs such as toilet facilities, etc. A system of either sharing the bathroom or properly allocating its use was necessary in order to maintain order and discipline among all of us and also to be sure that everyone was prepared, equipped and ready for school on time. It was expected of the older siblings to help the young ones with everything from eating and bathing to doing school homework, making their beds and organizing their rooms.

There was also the yearly ordeal of preparing to pay a visit to the family photographer for our annual family portrait. My father was ecstatically proud of his family of twelve children such that, rain or shine, his orders were to be obeyed for the annual "ritual" and anyone who disobeyed or did not cooperate would be severely punished. It meant a great deal to him and his pride of his family and of his twelve children. These family portraits had to be displayed all over the house for his sake!

Imagine the street scene created by my entire family marching along the 1-mile route to the neighborhood studio! Some of us felt embarrassed and very uneasy! Thereafter followed our procession back to our house, back to our piles of school homework and various household duties. After we survived the "ordeal", we would breathe a sigh of relief and return home to face other difficulties and challenges.

On a number of occasions, we had to make a head count of all the twelve children to be sure that no one was left behind in the outdoor park or an amusement park where the family went for an outing. It was not often that all the family would go anywhere with all the twelve children. Just the thought of inadequate transportation was good enough reason for our parents to discourage any such family outing to the beach, to watch a street opera or concert. It was just not an easy matter for obvious reasons.

It was in such an environment that we not only learnt to live together harmoniously, we were instilled by my parents with the age-old belief that family members must care deeply for one another and for the welfare of everyone. We were indeed a closely-knit family where the older siblings were expected to care for everyone, especially the young toddlers. Among the older siblings, somehow the burden often fell upon the shoulders of my elder sister Ruth to carry the responsibility of caring for the younger ones. Her sense of loving care and responsibility for her younger siblings seem to pervade her entire life– even to this day when she has to care for herself in her old age!

As poor as we were in those early days, my family could not afford to own a car or ride the public transportation. Without the convenience of either one of these, our usual mode of transportation was either to ride our bicycles or enjoy a ride on the rickshaw or trishaw (a 3-wheeled tricycle with a wooden carriage attached to the bicycle). The rickshaw or trishaw could only safely accommodate two adults or no more than 3 children. However, for the sake of economy and for lack of adequate financial means it became necessary to put as many as 6-7 of us kids in one rickshaw or trishaw! It meant that some of us had to sit on our laps while others had to sit on a wooden stool. This system worked fairly well except that on a rainy day we would have to cramp ourselves under the canvas-covered rickshaw – a great discomfort for everyone! Whether rain or shine, the boys had to ride their bicycles to our school some 5 miles away from home. There was no thought of our safety riding our bicycles on the busy public roads. Riding through the busy streets with other moving cars and bicycles, rickshaw and trishaws was truly a challenging experience. But we managed to cope pretty well with the hardships; our only thought being that we had to reach our school in time, even with having to struggle to ride the bicycle on the last stretch of a narrow and hilly road leading up to the school on Barker Road Hill. We used to envy those whose parents would send their children to school in a private chauffer-driven car!

In true tradition, we were taught and instilled with the thought that we must excel in every endeavor, whether it is our studies or developing our personal skills such as playing the piano. As such, my father and mother were often heard to say, "Have you finished your studies, reading and school work for today? Why are you not doing your studies and why are you wasting your time playing games?" To those who were musically inclined, they would say, "Have you been practicing your piano today or have you practiced playing those hymns you are supposed to play for this Sunday's Church service?" Inevitably, this last question usually was directed towards my elder sister Rebecca who was given the responsibility of being the official pianist for my father's church, as it was expected of her or, in her absence, one of my other sisters would have to be the substitute pianist for the church service.

In the matter of our academic studies, the thought of ever aspiring to higher college studies was out of the question. It was not a question of our intellectual ability or inclination more so than the family's limited financial resource. If anyone of us were to excel in studies and ever thought of going to college, especially to go for studies over-seas, my father would say, "Where are we going to find the means to send you overseas, and especially to go abroad for studies. You would have to take up a job first in order to earn enough money for such a venture. If you really want to go overseas for higher studies, even America, why don't you approach our missionary friends for assistance to find a good scholarship or financial assistance or write letters to apply for a scholarship?"

For most of us, this was exactly what we did in obedience to my father and what a blessing it was that all six of our twelve siblings managed to find our way to a college education in the USA! In my case, I was blessed with a 5-year college financial assistance through the generosity of a kind and loving Christian friend Mr. John E. Love – a friend of father's close missionary friend Dr. Dodsworth. Another one of father's missionary friend Dr. & Mrs. Paul Means secured a 4-year music scholarship for my sister Rebecca, who excelled in music, to study music at Wilamette University in Salem, Oregon. My sister Esther was awarded a Crusade Scholarship by the Methodist Church to study education at Scarritt College in Nashville, Tennessee while Peter, Joseph and Benjamin worked their way through college on "work-study" programs. When the family was financially able, we pulled our resources together to enable David to study Chemical Engineering in Melbourne, Australia.

Our early lives as "cheaper by the dozen" first generation of "Hang" siblings were filled with many interesting stories and experiences that are too numerous to elaborate. Our countless stories and experiences could fill the pages of some other book that could be entirely devoted to this subject. Some of our experiences and stories are related to my parents', especially of my father's life style of complete devotion and sacrifice to the Church and the well-being of their next of kin from mainland China.

One example of their "freely give and freely receive" life style is evident in their ever willingness to extend hospitality to many new immigrants from China, especially in their ministry to the church and to the Christian community. Even though my large family lived in tight quarters, my parents always had an open door" hospitality towards many new-comer friends and relatives – even to the extent that sometimes we had to surrender our bedroom to the visitors! There were occasions when some visitors were allowed to sleep in the church sanctuary for lack of enough beds or room space in our church parsonage. On other occasions these visitors were allowed to live with us (and even to share our meals at times!) for months on end with no regard for our own comfort or convenience. It was all done very naturally and sacrificially.

On a final note, I should say that living a life as a member of the "cheaper by the dozen" large family with twelve children had been most fascinating, rewarding as well as challenging in more ways than one! Thus the history of the "Hang" children of the late Rev. & Mrs. Paul S. H. Hang, Sr. has left a unique legacy for generations to come, and to cherish memories of everything that seemed uncommon in a normal family.

THE EVEN DOZEN "HANG" SIBLINGS

The Even Dozen Family Portrait – 1945

As we were in the 1940's: Mom & Dad with children (minus Ruth) in front of the Hinghwa Methodist Church – 1950

Family with 11ᵗʰ Child (Joseph) taken in 1942

Our Even "Dozen" Family portrait – 1949

CHAPTER 4
DAYS OF MY YOUTH

Living with father during my younger days was indeed a challenging one – truly, an experience of a life time and a lesson in strict parental obedience and self-discipline!

One may ask, "How was it like living with a father who loved his church and family, and expected complete obedience from all his children? What was it like to be one of twelve children that had to obey their father completely, never daring to do or say anything that would upset their father?" Such was the kind of life during my childhood when complete respect of and obedience to father was expected of everyone.

My father's complete dedication and commitment to the Church, particularly to the Hinghwa Methodist Church, in the early days of his ministry was truly remarkable and beyond question. In addition to his dedication to the ministry and his church building, my father cared deeply for the physical condition of the church and in so doing, he was very meticulous when it came to the church's upkeep. Being a man of strict discipline, he in turn instilled upon his children a deep sense of commitment to the proper upkeep and maintenance of the church property and its premises. On a typical Sunday morning, after praying in the church sanctuary, my father would survey the sanctuary in great detail, followed by a round of questions, "Has the floor been swept? Has anyone wiped the pews and all the furniture? Why are the chairs in the pews not arranged perfectly straight? Has anyone arranged the hymn books and placed the hymn numbers and psalms on the chalkboard?" Even the potted plants had to be properly pruned! If things weren't to his satisfaction, the blame was always put on the leader, that is, me.

His strong dedication and commitment also extended beyond his ministry. He expected his children to obey him and never to question his orders. My father was a perfectionist in his own way and, as such, there were certain ways that he expected things to be done, and that was the final word. Like many Oriental fathers of his time, his parenting style was somewhat authoritarian and punishment was inevitable for any disobedient child. How else could we not obey and respect him!

As a teenager, I often looked upon my father with fear and trembling, and that was the same feeling everyone had, especially when he was in a bad mood. He was a man with a strong will as well as a deep sense of morality and strict discipline. As an outstanding Chinese scholar, he possessed a wealth of knowledge and wisdom, and expected the same of his children. However, his expectations and standards were so high that not everyone was able to meet them.

My father also had high expectations of his children when it came to church attendance, whether it was a Sunday church service or a Wednesday night mid-week service or prayer meeting. If any of us was not in attendance or was late, we were always drilled with the same questions, "Who is not present for the Church service and why? No one is excused without my permission, especially without a good reason. And why are you not punctual?" If one of my sisters was the pianist for the church service that day, she had to be prepared and ready way in advance of the service. Strange as it may have seemed, there were times when the entire congregation consisted mainly of his children and wife when attendance was low because of his insistence that we all must be present at every church service or evening vesper.

My father was more relaxed in his retirement years, and I was able to develop a closer relationship with him. As young adults, we enjoyed doing all that we could to make his life more restful and enjoyable. He was often heard commenting that he was very contented and happy to enjoy his retirement in our Hong Kong Park residence, mostly provided by his children. He was visibly thankful for everything and devoted much of his time in prayer and meditation, as well as gardening, which was his hobby. He was also able to gather all the information he needed to write his autobiography entitled, "My Christian Testimony", thus leaving a legacy to the younger generations.

We were also greatly blessed with a loving and caring mother. She was truly a godly mother who cared deeply for everyone. She loved and nurtured all of her twelve children, and spared no effort to care for every child, especially those who had a special need. My mother perceived that I was one needing special attention, partly because of an illness I had at an early age and almost lost my life! As a result, others perhaps might have thought that mother cared more for me than her other children. As such, even when I was a young adult, my mother took it upon herself to constantly make sure that I had enough to eat and that I had taken my vitamins regularly. I also suffered from stomach ulcers and she always reminded me of my medications. My mother's attentiveness sometimes meant that I had to eat the eggs she had made for my breakfast, even if I was in a hurry to go to work.

For lack of proper words to correctly describe my mother and her mild-natured personality, a devoted wife to a preacher and loving mother to her twelve children, these words from the Book of Proverbs would appropriately describe some of her attributes:

Proverbs 31:20:   *"She stretches out her hands to the destitute, she reaches forth her hands to the poor"*

And

Proverbs 31:27: *"She looketh well to the ways of her household and eateth not the bread of idleness" She lived to a rightful old age of 75 yrs!*

My mother reluctantly left the comfort of her family mansion in China when she married my father and followed him to his Christian ministry in the far-away land of Singapore. She was known to be a soft-spoken woman with a deep love of family that was often seen in the Oriental tradition. Coming from a relatively well-do-do landowner family in China, she was a woman of patience and long-suffering as she faithfully played her role as a loving wife and helpmate to her husband. She had successfully raised all her twelve children and always remembered everyone's birthday when she would prepare a special 'breakfast with two eggs' for the birthday child. She deeply loved Jesus and her husband's ministry, and devoted much time and energy to serve God as well. To me, she was truly a special mother, although she dearly loved all her 12 children!

CHAPTER 5
SURVIVING WORLD WAR II

This is a brief account of our narrow escapes from the devastations of World War II, while living in Singapore during 1940-42.It is also about our hardships and bitter experiences as young children in the aftermath of the Japanese invasion of Singapore.

The year was 1940 when Singapore surrendered to the Japanese Imperial forces, which had invaded South East Asia and captured Singapore during World War II. The Japanese had driven the British and Allied Forces out of Singapore and had gained control of our country. Many had evacuated from Singapore but, unfortunately, my family was left behind to suffer the pain and hardships under the Japanese occupation and rule.

Our bitter experiences and vivid impressions of those treacherous war years had left an indelible mark in our memories. My youngest brother, Benjamin, was only an infant and my eldest sister, Mary, was sixteen. It seemed unfair and cruel that young innocent lives were put in harms' way as we experienced the horror and tragedies of a major world war that caused large-scale destruction to Singapore.

During the critical days before the Japanese invasion, warning sirens were often heard, indicating the imminent danger of invasion and approaching enemy warplanes. As the sirens grew louder and clearer, we knew that the enemy warplanes were about to strike and that we had to take cover to save our lives! Adults could be heard shouting, "Hurry up, run for the underground shelter! Don't waste time! The warplanes are coming and enemy bombs may drop on us anytime! You may get killed if you do not get into the underground shelter right away!"

We had built an underground shelter on a vacant piece of land, adjacent to the shop house church at No. 27 Sam Leong Road. The shelter measured about 10 feet wide by 30 feet long and was 4 feet below ground level, and was covered with sandbags placed on top of a wooden-frame for support. The underground shelter would protect us from any flying shrapnel from the explosive bombs, but it would not save us if we were hit directly by a bomb. As soon as warplanes were sighted, the sirens would go off, causing our hearts to beat fast as we scrambled into the underground shelter. Once inside the shelter, we were instructed to lay low on straw mats which had been placed on the ground, either to try to sleep or keep absolutely quiet until the danger was over.

Our parents worried that we might get killed if an enemy bomb would hit us directly, so they looked for safer shelter for us to escape to, away from the city. Fortunately, a close friend of the family, Dr. T. H. Ling, had a house in the Newton area, which was outside the city and was hidden by many trees. He offered us shelter at his home temporarily while the city was heavily bombed by the Japanese warplanes.

We felt much safer at Dr. Ling's residence than in the underground shelter, away from our church parsonage home, which was located in the crowded part of the city. A number of other families also took shelter at Dr. Ling's residence, so while some of us took shelter in the lower level of the house, others hid in the underground shelter located behind the house which was camouflaged by lots of fruit trees.

Not long after, we received news that our church parsonage

home had suffered major damage from a bomb that was dropped next to the church building. We were very thankful to the Lord that we had left just in time for Dr. Ling's Newton residence. We could have been killed or seriously hurt had we remained at our parsonage home when the bomb had fallen next to the house at No.27 Sam Leong Road.

In order not to inconvenience the Lings longer than was needed, my parents came up with another plan to move us to yet another location, this time to the home of another close family friend, Mr. Sie, on Madras Lane. Although in the city, his house was a tall brick structure, with the front of the building reinforced with yet another protective brick wall. While enemy warplanes rained numerous bombs over the city and killed many, we felt safe in the Sie residence. We were thankful to the Sies for sheltering us and other church families in their home.

Soon after Singapore surrendered to the Japanese Imperial forces in 1941, we returned to our home at No. 27 Sam Leong Road. By then, it had been determined that the building was safe for us to move back into. The explosive force of the bomb that had fallen near the building created a huge gaping hole, thus weakening the wall of the building facing the vacant land. In order to stabilize the damaged wall, wooden props were erected to strengthen the wall, making it safe for us to live in it before major repairs were made.

Of the many terrifying experiences during the time of the Japanese occupation, one frightening episode remains vivid in my mind. A drunken Japanese soldier had knocked at our front door. Too afraid to open the door, we waited to look out the window until he had left, and was shocked by what we saw. Out on the five-foot wide concrete sidewalk just outside our front door was a dead human body! We immediately reported it to the police and were told later that the man had apparently died of suicide!

While the Japanese occupied Singapore, communication systems, especially the media, were very limited and we had great difficulty keeping ourselves informed on the latest news. By Japanese decree, no one was allowed to possess any wireless equipment, not even a radio, so we were literally cut off from the rest of the world. If any were found, they were confiscated and the culprit would be severely punished.

When the Japanese finally surrendered in 1944, after the Allied Forces had taken over the Pacific Area, there was much jubilation in Singapore and all over Asia. We were thankful that the war had finally ended and it was finally peaceful again. As we reflect upon all the events that impacted our lives during those war years, we have much to be thankful for, especially for God's protection and provision during that time.

CHAPTER 6
A QUESTION OF SURVIVAL

This is the story of our traumatic experiences and struggles, of how we survived the horrors of World War II during 1941 – 1944 in Singapore. All twelve of us were very young, the eldest being Mary at the age of 16, and the youngest, Benjamin. As the fifth child, I was only 9 years old then.

Soon after the Japanese enemy invaded Singapore and took control of our lives, one of their first acts of atrocity was the mass murder of thousands of innocent young men for no apparent reason other than the fact that they were Chinese and perhaps young professionals who were Chinese or British subjects. All these young men were taken away from their homes and loved ones, only to be put in quarantine camps to be interrogated, physically abused and many were executed!

It was rumored in later years that, for whatever reason, the Japanese soldiers were ordered by the Imperial Japanese Emperor to exterminate young Chinese men as a form of revenge towards the Chinese people for their past evil deeds. My father was one of those taken into the quarantine station. As he relayed what it was like, he would tell us of how the men had to stand in long lines, waiting in the hot sun to get past the check point. My father said, "Every young man was interrogated and the majority of them were taken away in open-ended trucks, never to be seen or heard from again." Their families were left destitute, not knowing the fate of their loved ones. Only years later, it was discovered that thousands were slaughtered and buried in mass graves in the remote parts of Singapore Island. As a young man in his thirties, my father's life was miraculously spared. As he recollected, "I just clasped the Bible against my chest, hoping that the Japanese soldier could see that I was a 'holy' man, and that I was not their target victim".

As young children, we were spared the agony of being interrogated and quarantined, but our greatest concern was the fear of starvation since essential foodstuff was seriously lacking, and there was also the fear of life-threatening diseases. We lived without any significant resources, not even basic foods such as rice, salt and sugar, which were very scarce. Whatever food there was were channeled to feed the Japanese. Those that owned any vacant plots of land resorted to cultivating whatever potatoes or vegetable they could grow to supplement the little rice and sugar rationed to them by the Japanese war administration. My family tried to do that, but without any success!

The war years left a lasting impression on our young minds. When we ran out of food, my father ingeniously found a way to place my elder brother, Peter, and I in an orphanage, although we were not legally orphans. In our large family of twelve children, that meant having two less mouths to feed! Coming from a closely-knit family and never ever having left home, we were not accustomed to living away from home. That painful and short sojourn at the orphanage traumatized Peter and I such that we could not sleep at night. We cried our hearts out and were very homesick. Living conditions at the orphanage were miserably uncomfortable and unbearable. We stayed in crowded quarters, slept on hard wooden floors and for the most part had no idea what was happening or what had happened to our family and loved ones. .

Although we stayed at the orphanage for only a short while, the days were very long and monotonous, with nothing to do except to sleep and stare into space. We were not allowed to read books or play with any toys and the days seemed to drag on and last forever. Besides the endless boredom, we were always hungry and it seemed like a very long time between meals. Even the smell of food from the kitchen was ever so delightful to our senses as mealtime approached!

We were fed three small meals a day and they never satisfied our small appetites. Breakfast consisted of just a slice of plain white bread and a cup of diluted and unsweetened tea, usually given to us late in the morning after a long and hungry night. Still hungry, we were starved by lunchtime when we were given only a small bowl of watery porridge with a sprinkling of cooked sweet potato leaves and very little steamed or fried fish. Dinner was just as skimpy with a small bowl of steamed rice, potato and steamed or fried fish. We were malnourished and very underweight and skinny when we left the orphanage.

Soon after surviving our ordeal at the orphanage, Peter and I were put to work in a bicycle factory on Rochore Road. We were only ten and twelve years old. Peter had to work on the shop floor and I worked in the office, serving coffee and cleaning the office for two Japanese generals who managed the bicycle manufacturing shop. All able men were forced to work in some form of industry or occupation. Even girls were ordered to work in order for the economy to recover from the devastations of the war. In exchange for our work, we were paid with Japanese-made cigarettes instead of money, which we in turn sold them to get some money to help our family.

As a young ten-year old and at a very impressionable age, it bothered me terribly to witness some of the Japanese atrocities and their very cruel forms of punishment for any wrongdoing. The workers were to obey strict orders, failing which they would be severely punished. If one failed to obey orders, instead of being terminated, he would be physically inflicted with pain, usually in the form of slapping, until he bled in the face. On one occasion, I witnessed the Japanese factory manager inflict physical punishment on a worker until he had passed out and had to be carried away by his fellow workers. The factory workers were punished sometimes for the most insignificant reason, either of a disciplinary nature or because of bad job performance.

Quite unexpectedly, a strange development took place that caused me to run away from the factory. The Japanese General possessed a death-defying long sword, which was the Japanese symbol of a high-ranking official, and he used it with great skill. Before then, I had heard stories of a Japanese soldier's great skill with his sword, being able to kill a person with one swing of his sword, decapitating a person's head. I had even heard of a human head floating in the city canal, the result of being killed by a Japanese soldier. I was told one day, through an interpreter, that the Japanese General liked me very much, and that he had expressed interest in adopting me as a son. A sudden wave of fear overwhelmed me, afraid that the Japanese General might someday use his sword to hurt or kill me! As a young boy, the thought of being adopted by the General and the fear of him cutting off my head when he was angry caused me to panic! My immediate reaction to the interpreter's proposal was to run for my life, notwithstanding the office boy's job! I cared nothing for the job at that moment, but for the safety of my life! Looking back, if I had not run away, I could very well have been adopted by the Japanese General and perhaps be another cruel Japanese general.

In order to help our family survive the deprivations of the war, we had to be creative in finding ways to earn a little extra money to help with the family budget. One way was to sell unwanted household items at the local flea market by the roadside in the hot and humid tropical sun. Sometimes, those at home would make delicious fried fish cakes with shrimp topping, while the boys like Peter and I would peddle our bicycles to nearby shops and opium dens to try and sell the cakes to anybody, including the lazy rickshaw pullers who were smoking opium in the den. As children, little did we know of the dangers of opium addiction or of being arrested for entering an opium den!

One of the many things we did to survive was to raise ducks and chicken which fed on leftover food or food that was stale. We were thrilled whenever a chicken laid an egg. We also tried, unsuccessfully, to raise a couple of pigs that died because we were not able to feed them properly. Furthermore, we tried growing our own vegetables on a small plot of land in front of the house that was about 4 feet by 12 feet, but with disappointing results! These were but some of the things we did to supplement our family's limited food supply during the war years.

What else did we experience during those war years that had left a deep impression upon our young minds – of what we had to do in order to survive the war years? The country was in a state of chaos, the least of which was the shortage of essential food supply that was our basic need besides water and electricity.

As young children, we did not have the luxury of ample food supply. The fact that there were twelve of us hungry kids must have been really difficult for our parents to find sufficient food to feed all of us. Such was the scenario when we received the welcome news that the American Red Cross and Salvation Army had food and clothing donations from America that would be rationed to needy folks such as we were.

Imagine our great excitement and relief when we were able to receive some needed foodstuff and clothing from the Red Cross and the Salvation Army. We knew very little about America then and we were simply thrilled to be given such "delicacies" (to us, it seems) as Spam luncheon meat, Libby's canned vegetables and fruits, even some generic type canned food such as corned beef, etc. We were even happy to be given chocolates and various candy, even clothing that needed alteration to fit our small Asian sizes. In those days, our only clothing were the home-made kind, mostly hand made by my mother with the help of the older girls. For us to survive the wartime economy meant having just the basic essential foodstuffs such as rice, some flour, vegetables or fish. Even a dash of salt or soy sauce was not always required seasoning for our food because many such essential items were in short supply. It was in that kind of environment that we thought to ourselves that the foodstuffs and clothing we benefited from the American Red Cross and the Salvation Army were "heaven sent" for which we were truly grateful.

It reached a point when there was a critical shortage of food supply and my entire family was forced by the Japanese administration to move away from Singapore. Many fled to nearby countries like Burma or India. We were given orders to evacuate the city and if we did not obey the orders to leave the city, we were told we would starve or even die from malnutrition. We had no choice but to obey and were relocated to the remote jungles of Endau, in Johore, Malaysia.

When the day came for us to leave, we were picked up in open-ended trucks and were allowed to bring only our essential belongings. During our travel to Endau, we learned that it was to be a dangerous, life-threatening drive on narrow roads through the jungles of Johore, Malaysia. We were told later that the jungles were infested with desperate bandits who would plunder our caravan, kill the Japanese soldiers escorting us, and seize all the goods in the trucks. Their intention was to kill the Japanese soldiers but to spare the lives of the others. Unfortunately, it put all of our lives in danger of being killed as well. In the melee, many were killed but we managed to escape death by the grace and mercy of God! Six of the trucks in our 8-vehicle caravan were seized except the two vehicles in which we were traveling!

We lived in Endau as farmers, tilling the soil and growing our own produce. We ended up living in that remote jungle for a year while struggling to survive. Many basic needs were lacking and there was not even proper sanitation other than a communal outhouse. As the soil in Endau was very lean and no fertilizer was available, we had to carry buckets of sanitary waste to the farm every morning. We were glad to return to civilization when the war ended. Upon returning home to Singapore, life slowly returned to normal in the city with the whole process of rebuilding and reconstruction.

It was indeed a "Question of Survival" for our whole family, as we were subjected to much suffering and hardships in the hands of the occupying Japanese administration. Life in those days was very chaotic, to say the least, and many resorted to making money through illicit trade deals and cheating. Regardless of age and gender, everyone was compelled to engage in some kind of work or preoccupation to survive the extreme hardships. For some, that was the only way for them to survive the devastations following the great destructions and hardships of a major world war.

These are but just a few of the many stories that could be related (or written) of our traumatic experiences during the World War II years, truly a "Question of Survival"! In retrospect, I believe that God's hand was upon us, protecting and sustaining us throughout the dangerous and momentous years.

CHAPTER 7
SAILING ON THE HIGH SEAS

The expression, "The Slow Boat to China" became a reality for us during our voyage across the high seas in 1952. However, it was the "Slow Boat to New York" that my sister Rebecca and I were sailing in across the oceans. The boat ride took us across the Indian and Atlantic Oceans and the Mediterranean Sea. Along the way, our ship stopped at Belawan Deli in Sumatra, Cochin, Calcutta, Port Said, Gibraltar, Halifax, and Boston before finally landing in New York. Altogether, the trip lasted five long weeks!

Our entire family and many friends were at the dock in the Singapore harbor to bid us farewell, two young and aspiring students, when we left for America for further studies. The freighter, the S.S. "Steel Chemist" was to take us on our long voyage to the U.S.A. Many were visibly in tears and giving us kisses and hugs, not knowing when we would meet again. Only a few days before our departure were we singing the song, "God be with you till we meet again! Till we meet!...Till we meet!...God be with you till we meet again!" at an emotional farewell party hosted by our Church Youth Fellowship. .

When our ship arrived at a seaport in Sumatra a few days later, there was a "dock strike", so we were stranded in the

Indonesian port of Belawan for several days, waiting for the cargo to be unloaded. With nothing else to do while the ship was in port, we took short walks along the wharf but we were warned never to stray too far away from the ship and risk being left behind in a strange place. When the strike was finally over, we felt a sigh of relief when our ship sailed on to Cochin, India but we were unaware of the very rough seas and high waves of the Indian Ocean yet to come!

Sailing the Indian Ocean was quite an experience, one that we had never experienced before! The S.S. "Steel Chemist" was a 17,000-ton freighter, carrying mostly raw rubber to the U.S.A. and we had to endure the awful smell of raw rubber that permeated the entire ship except when strong winds were blowing! When we were in the middle of the Indian Ocean, we were pounded by huge high waves of 8-10 feet and washing over the deck. It caused the ship to rock back and forth precariously, and things to roll all over the ship. We thought that we were headed for a shipwreck! In the midst of this, the ship's crew member shouted to us, "Get off the deck or you may be thrown overboard!" It was safer for us "un-seaworthy" folks to remain below deck while the ship was rocking about dangerously. As we stayed in the safety of our cabins below, we could hear the crashing of dishes and glassware in the dining room, and the clanging of pots and pans in the kitchen!

As everyone sought shelter either in their cabins, on the upper deck or in the watertight areas below the deck, the only visible crew members above deck were either steering the ship in the elevated control room or men working on the deck to safeguard the ship's equipment and precious cargo. While some tried to sleep in their cabins, the movement of the ship caused others to get sea sick and throw up. Along with the chief officer, some of us chose to take long walks on the decks, which helped us overcome the sea-sickness and keep our bodies from throwing out our meals!

Other than that, we were treated royally at mealtime. The freighter normally had no more than 12 fee-paying passengers and we had our meals with the ship's crew in the captain's dining room. Although it was a semi-formal event, the captain chose to follow the British-style etiquette and required everyone to wear proper attire and act like guests. For my friends and I, that was our first exposure to the "western" cuisine, which was very rich compared to the Asian food and too much for our small appetites. As a result, we put on quite a bit of weight to our small Asian bodies when the voyage was over. It was hard to imagine a skinny young man like me boarding the ship at just a mere 98 lbs. and leaving it weighing 115 lbs at the end of the voyage, gaining over 15 lbs in just 5 weeks! Unfortunately, for those of our fellow passengers who had gotten seasick, not only did they manage to survive the sea voyage, but they also seemed to have lost some pounds instead. They even enjoyed the voyage in spite of the ordeal!

Unlike most passenger liners, the S.S. "Steel Chemist" freighter had very little recreational or entertainment facilities. In order to kill the boredom, we were provided with plenty of books and reading materials in the lounge area. While some tried to keep busy by listening to the radio broadcasts, others would follow the ship's crew in doing endless miles of walking exercises on the deck as a means to overcome the sea-sickness.

For most of us young Asian passengers, sailing on the high seas that spanned nearly half the globe was an exciting adventure! We enjoyed looking out at the vast expanse of oceans, and someone would spot a school of sharks or whales every now and then. Some even suggested dropping a fishing pole and to try their hand at fishing!

Whenever the ship approached another port, we would be waiting on the deck anxiously checking out the next port of call and making plans to go ashore to explore the new place. As we approached the Indian city of Calcutta, fellow passengers would point out the numerous Hindhu temples and the strange looking people. Some would gather alongside the ship, looking for handouts or hoping to sell us their wares or anything.

As we sailed through the Red Sea, we saw endless stretches of desert sand and camels working as "beasts of prey" in the Egyptian landscape. Traveling across the Suez Canal into the Mediterranean Sea was quite an educational experience for us, as we moved through a series of water-locked gates and navigation systems to cross the Canal.

Sailing the calm Mediterranean Sea was relatively peaceful, as we enjoyed lots of good food and relaxation. We sun-bathed during the day and enjoyed the cool weather in the evenings. Everyone was very excited as we approached the port of Gibraltar. That was our departing point from the Mediterranean Sea into the Atlantic Ocean. Unlike the Indian Ocean, the Atlantic Ocean was relatively calm so the weeklong voyage from Gibraltar to Halifax, Nova Scotia was very pleasurable. We finally reached our final destination, New York, and thus ending our 5-week long adventure on the high seas!

CHAPTER 8
"THOSE WERE THE DAYS!"

For most people, memories of their younger days in college or university will always be fondly remembered and cherished. Out of our twelve children, Peter, Rebecca and I were the first to be blessed with the good fortune of experiencing the American way of life as foreign students during 1951- 1957.This chapter describes our memories of the great adventures and the challenges to pursue the "American Dream".

For us, our adventures and cherished memories of the time while studying in America was an experience of a lifetime, and it also brought us closer together as siblings. We saw America as the land of great opportunity while pursuing our higher education. For us, the experience was truly like a long-awaited dream come true.

We left Singapore by ship, sailing through the Indian and Atlantic Oceans, and finally landing in New York after five long weeks. Never having traveled abroad, we were ecstatic about experiencing the thrill and excitement of "seeing the world", and of visiting many famous cities and "wonders of the world" we had only heard about, such as Boston. New York, Wash, DC, Chicago, the Statue of Liberty and Niagara Falls, etc.

When we first arrived in New York, we were greeted by the Statue of Liberty. What an awesome sight it was! To a bystander, we seemed like ignorant tourists, I said to my sister, "Wow! Look at the Statue of Liberty! It is really awesome! Is that the Empire State Building, the tallest building in the world?" Every sight was just breathtaking. We and our three other shipmates decided to tour the world famous New York City. We visited museums and had our first taste of the "American fast food" i.e. McDonald's hamburger, French fries and popcorn. The change in climate, from the tropical heat and humidity of Singapore to the temperate climate in America, was a very welcome relief!

We had our first taste of the American Chinese food, such as "Chop Suey" and "Chow Mien", in Chinatown, New York. We had not had Chinese food since we left home many weeks ago, so that even Chop Suey tasted great! We missed Chinese food so much that one of our friends suggested that we find someplace where Rebecca could make us some real Chinese food, like fried rice or fried noodles.

As we had very little money, we decided to take advantage of the great deals offered by Greyhound Bus to travel to Washington, D.C., Chicago, and then out west to Seattle, Washington. At Washington, D.C., again, we were the typical tourists, as we marveled at the majestic U.S. Capitol Building, with the gorgeous looking domed roof! We also visited the Lincoln Memorial, the famous White House and other tourist attractions that we had heretofore only heard and read about.

Besides being captivated by the interesting sights of the big cities, we were also introduced to the American way of life. Although we were enjoying checking out new places, it was quite a culture shock for us in this strange new land. We had each other but we felt homesick for our many loved ones and friends whom we had left behind in Singapore, as well as the taste of our familiar home-cooked Chinese food.

We were greeted in Chicago by a missionary friend, Miss Ellen Suffern, who had served in our home Church. She took us to her home near Lake Michigan and said, "How wonderful to see you again after so many years since I was last in Singapore as a missionary. By the way, how are your parents? Do you have enough warm clothing?" I thought it very thoughtful of her to ask that since we were not accustomed to the cool temperate climate in the United States. Miss Suffern was a great host, taking us to the Art Museum, the Science and Industry Museum, the Aquarium, the Planetarium, and she even drove us around on a sightseeing tour of the windy city. She had also gotten us tickets for a rare treat to see the world famous Holiday On Ice show at the Chicago Stadium. We enjoyed two very busy and enjoyable days with her in Chicago.

After Chicago, we boarded the Amtrak train for Minneapolis and Seattle, Washington. In Minneapolis, we visited with another former missionary friend, Miss Ruth Harvey. She remembered that we were two of the twelve Rev. Hang's children and that we were her favorite Sunday School students in Singapore. It had been quite a long time since we had seen her. She was also very generous and after asking about our college, she gave us $100 when we left, which was a lot to us because we had very little.

Then followed our 2-day train ride from Minneapolis to Seattle, traveling west through the gorgeous prairies, the vast farmland and the Rocky Mountains. The sights were both gorgeous and breathtaking! We were so excited to experience the long train ride and not wanting to miss anything, were reluctant to sleep except to take occasional naps! We had little money for food, but were happy to have sandwiches and snacks to keep us from being too hungry.

When we arrived in Seattle, we were met by a couple of elderly ladies, a mother and daughter, who were friends of my father's good old missionary friends, Dr. & Mrs. M. Dodsworth. They took us to their home in Tacoma where we settled down and rested well from the long cross-country train ride. They then showed us the campus of the College of Puget Sound, where I was to enroll for college. We were treated so well that we had momentarily forgotten about feeling homesick!

Although we were enjoying the new and exciting American way of life, we still felt like "strangers in paradise", so it was good that Rebecca and I had each other to lean on. For a whole month since we had left Singapore, Rebecca and I had grown very close, as we traveled and shared similar experiences. Alas! The time had come for us to part. Rebecca was to leave for Wilamette University in Salem, Oregon, and as I bade her good-bye at the Greyhound Bus depot, I again felt a sudden surge of homesickness and loneliness. Here I was, trying to overcome the initial culture shock of living in a strange new country and finding myself all alone and having to say good bye to my dear sister.

When school started, the busyness of adjusting to college life and participating in campus and church activities helped me overcome the feeling of homesickness and loneliness. However, the long weekends and in-between semester breaks made me long to get together with Rebecca. Whenever any of my new-found friends from overseas were homesick and wanted to get away for a weekend, I was quick to reply, "We could drive to Salem, which is only 20 miles away, to visit Rebecca and her Asian college friends." Of course, everyone thought it was a great idea. My friends and I looked forward to eating a nice Chinese meal and hanging out with our Asian friends. "Maybe, your sister could even make us some home-cooked Chinese food," one of my friends suggested. Before long, those weekends became regular outings we all looked forward to.

The long summer vacations were packed with many exciting events and activities besides working part-time on odd jobs to earn some needed pocket money. Rebecca's first summer was spent meeting her scholarship sponsors at the various Wesleyan Service Guilds in all of Oregon. She gave talks about life in Asia and was often asked to entertain group meetings by playing the piano, much to the delight of her sponsors who adored her

My first summer in America was spent with a group of international students in a fruit orchard at Milton-Freewater, in Washington State. While some students were sent out to work in the fruit-canning factory, I joined others in picking cherries in the cherry orchards. It was fun eating the delicious cherries while picking them. We were paid for picking cherries based on the pounds of cherries that we had picked. But it was hard work standing on a ladder, reaching out to the cherry tree branches, and putting the cherries in a bucket strung over our shoulders in the hot summer heat!

However, it was not all hard work though. There were times for fellowship and we also enjoyed an occasional evening campfire. After a meal of barbeque hot dogs and hamburger, we sometimes sat around the campfire singing songs, sharing and eating roasted marshmallows, late into the evening. We had a great time of fellowship.

Towards the end of the summer vacation, our good friends of the family, Dr. and Mrs. Paul Means, invited me to their home in Eugene, Oregon to spend the rest of the summer in their home. There, Dr. Means would share things with me about Singapore and Malaysia, while Mrs. Means showed me how she cared for her flower gardens. She could also make great tasting Singapore curry and Asian dishes, a real treat for me

Rebecca and I were invited to spend a few of our Thanksgiving and Christmas vacations with Dr. and Mrs. Means in their home in Eugene, Oregon. We were also able to spend one Christmas with the Dodsworth's family in their home in Bellingham, Washington. For the first time, we were introduced to the traditional American Christmas, with real American food and Christmas gifts. We also experienced our first snow fight with their son, Paul, whose beautiful wedding I was privileged to attend! Dr. Dodsworth was instrumental in securing the needed college financial assistance for me that was offered by his college roommate Mr. John E. Love, for which I am truly thankful.

The summer of 1954 was really special for Peter, Rebecca and I. My brother Peter was studying at Baldwin-Wallace College in Berea, Ohio. He took it upon himself to make plans for our second summer together. Being a very social person and having many Christian friends, Peter said to Rebecca and I, "How would you like to come out East and join me for a summer job? "We could spend the summer working together at the Lakeside Resort on Lake Erie." He had even arranged for the three of us to work in a restaurant at this resort where free accommodation and meals would be provided. Peter said, "Paul and I could both be dish washers while Rebecca could work as a cashier at this restaurant." We thought Peter's plan sounded too good to be true. It meant a great opportunity for us to travel East to Ohio, as well as a wonderful reunion for the three of us! The thought of the three of us being together for the summer was comforting to me.

For two months, we labored hard at our jobs. We were thankful for the opportunity to work together as well as earn some pocket money. We especially enjoyed the days when the business was not too busy. The restaurant manager would say, "You could take the day off and enjoy walking around the Resort, swim in Lake Erie or just relax by the beautiful Lakeside resort beach.

By the end of our 2-month job assignment, we still had another month left to the summer vacation. Then Peter suggested, "We can visit Cleveland where I have some friends, and maybe even go see the big tourist city of Chicago." Everyone was in favor of it and we all had a great time in Chicago working on part time jobs and even acting as tourists. After a wonderful summer together, we had to sadly leave Peter in Ohio and to return to our colleges in Eugene and Salem, Oregon.

When the opportunity arose, Peter and I decided to complete our college degrees together at Oregon State College in order to help one another emotionally and financially. We thought that by sharing the cost of renting an apartment and making our own meals, we could minimize our college expenses. By then, my old 1948 Ford two-door car needed to be replaced, as I could never get it started unless I parked it on a slope and jump-started the engine. With money saved, we were able to purchase two second hand cars, a 1952 Chevrolet and, a 1953 Chevrolet, both cars costing less than $300.00 each.

We decided to spend Thanksgiving 1955 sightseeing in Vancouver, Washington. Being unfamiliar with driving in snow and ice, while on our way back from Vancouver (near Everett, WA) our car skidded out of control on the roadway and landed in a ditch along the shoulder! Fortunately, God sent a kind and helpful stranger to help pull us out of the ditch. We were both unhurt but badly shaken. That was a painful lesson for us two young and ignorant Asian students from Singapore!

Rebecca graduated the summer of 1957 and it was time to send her back home to Singapore, this time by plane! I graduated the following year and being young and enthusiastic, together with a Thai classmate friend, I drove 18 hours to San Francisco to look for a job! There, I was blessed with an Engineering Assistant's position with the Company, International Engineering Inc., where I worked for two years. I had the opportunity to work with an engineering team, in designing and managing two hydroelectric projects -- the TVA Brownlee Dam and the Oxley Dam in Idaho. I got to work on a very interesting project, that is, in designing the "fish ladder" for the two hydroelectric power dams. With a good job and a handsome salary, I was able to send monthly checks to my parents in Singapore to help them with buying a house for them to live in their retirement. My parents were blessed and thrilled to enjoy a lovely home.

My brother Peter graduated with two degrees, a Bachelor of Science and a Master of Science in 1959 when he decided to join me in San Francisco. However, when my job situation appeared uncertain, I said to Peter, "I think it is time that we return home to Singapore" We had been away from home for seven long years and never had the opportunity nor the means to make a trip back home during all those years. After careful consideration, and seeing that Peter was not in good health, we decided that it was to our best interest to return home to Singapore.

So, on a cool summer day in July 1959, Peter and I boarded the S.S. "President Cleveland" in San Francisco and, after a relaxing ten-days' journey sailing across the Pacific Ocean, we set foot in Hong Kong. My parents were in Hong Kong enjoying a long-overdue holiday and awaiting our arrival! Although we were simply overjoyed and cried when we saw our parents again after seven long years, we felt like total strangers. As we hugged each other, my parents' commented, "Is that really you, Paul? You look so different now, somewhat Americanized!" Having not spoken in the Hinghwa dialect for so long, we were unable to communicate properly, except with some gestures or body language. But that did not stop us from spending a few wonderful days together in Hong Kong, before sailing back to Singapore. It was a wonderful time of reunion for the four of us, as we enjoyed the sights in Hong Kong and our time of reunion.

THOSE WERE THE DAYS

Rebecca & Paul Jr. before leaving Singapore – 1952

Brothers Joseph & Benjamin visiting Esther in Buffalo, New York – 1962

Large gathering of relatives and friends at our wedding in 1965

Father and Mother vacationed in Hong Kong in 1959 when Paul returned from U.S.

Paul Jr. met Benjamin at Indianapolis - 1977

CHAPTER 9
OUR CHILDREN: THE WONDERFUL YEARS

We are a family with 4 children, a son and 3 daughters, and we lived those wonderful years in Singapore when our children grew up in a world filled with fond memories.

My wife, Doris, and I were married in January 1965 at a grand wedding attended by many relatives and friends. The beautiful Church ceremony was followed by two large dinner receptions, one in Singapore and another in Kuala Lumpur, Malaysia. I was then working for Exxon in Malaysia, so after our wedding, I had to return to Malaysia and Doris remained in Singapore when she was expecting our first child. Both Mom and daughter joined me in our new home in Kuala Lumpur after Debbie was born on October 12, 1965. When our second daughter, Phoebe, was due, we decided it was best for her also to be born in Singapore and to be cared for by my wife's mother.

Our daughter Phoebe entered the world on March 7, 1967. I continued to work for Exxon in Malaysia and traveled frequently between Singapore and Malaysia to visit my family. Malaysia was not our permanent home and we were Singapore citizens, so we wanted our children to keep their Singapore citizenship. We wanted them to grow up in Singapore where they would be given a good education and not worry about what would become of their future. For this to happen, I had to commute back and forth between Singapore and Malaysia for a season for the sake of our children's education and for them to enjoy the same citizenship benefits we did as Singaporeans.

After the racial riots erupted in Malaysia in 1969, we decided to move back to Singapore after our son, Timothy, was born. He is our third child, born on January 19, 1970.

We had many unforgettable experiences with our children living in Malaysia. Debbie and Phoebe had Sunday School friends who celebrated their birthdays with them, and Debbie was even pampered by our neighbors, the Gong's, who took a liking to her. Living in one of Malaysia's premier new townships in Petaling Jaya was like a sojourn in a country estate, away from the crowded, bustling city of Kuala Lumpur.

From Malaysia, we made frequent trips by car to Singapore during the holidays and weekends to visit friends and relatives. On other occasions, we would drive up to the hilltop mountain resorts of Faber Hills or Cameron Highlands to enjoy the cool mountain air and relax, and enjoy meals prepared for us! Then on January 25, 1971, our daughter, Muriel, was born, also in Singapore. For a short season, we lived with my parents in their Hong Kong Park residence before we bought our own home at Faber Hills, on the west coast of Singapore. That was like a new beginning for us living in a nice new home.

In 1971, we moved into our next home at Saunders Road that was closer to the city. My father had passed away in 1972 and my mother needed our company, so she moved in with us. I was working at the Far East Shipbuilding shipyard in Jurong and it was quite a long daily commute to work. We were blessed with the luxury of a full-time maid that enabled my wife to return to work as a Dental Nurse at the Methodist Girls' School. Our daughter Debbie started to attend school at the same place that Doris worked and our three younger children went to the Khee Fatt Kindergarten, within walking distance from our Saunders Road home.

Our children had many aunts and uncles to pamper them, and were blessed with enjoying constant attention and lots of goodies. We had frequent family gatherings, as we relished sumptuous home-cooked cuisine and rousing family activities. Imagine what it was like in large gatherings of relatives and friends at a birthday party or anniversary with lots of tasty food. Our Chinese Lunar New Year falls on a different date every year, often not the same date as January 1st. The children always looked forward to it, saying, "When is Chinese New Year going to be this year? Where are we going for our big New Year's Eve dinner?" They were also pampered with new clothes and new shoes for Chinese New Year was always a time of happy family gatherings, laughter and enjoyment.

Our children loved having pets, but we did not have much luck raising either dogs or cats. First of all, both my wife and I had little interest in dogs and cats and secondly, Doris was fearful of them. However, a friend of mine got me interested in breeding parakeets in our Petaling Jaya home in Malaysia and it became a fun hobby for all to watch them play and mate. I made my own bird cage and enjoyed watching the parakeets as they frolicked and grew into beautiful young parakeets of many different colors.

Living in Singapore was both exciting and fascinating for our children. In addition to the frequent family gatherings and events, we had our family outings to the beach or parks such as the Jurong Bird Park and the well-known tourist attractions such as the Botanical Gardens. They even got to experience artificial snow produced by a machine to thrill them at a shopping center! I had my regular bowling session on our Saturday outing followed by a treat to "dim sum" lunch even after our Sunday worship.

Our Sundays in Singapore were especially enjoyable, filled with many social activities in addition to the children attending Sunday school and worship services. We have fond memories of our years in our own home at Faber Hills as well as Jalan

Merlimau, off of Thomson Road. Being little children, they were very creative and they indulged in creating their own "make believe" mini dramas while enjoying the outdoors in our spacious garden. We were even blessed with a tall papaya tree produced delicious, sweet papayas in our yard.

Before our big move to America, we lived at our Winstedt Road home near the city. We experienced many interesting and exciting events that made our lives in Singapore truly memorable. Those were the "Wonderful Years of Our Children", living in Singapore before we left to emigrate to the United States of America in 1983.

CHAPTER 10
SURVIVING THE RACIAL RIOTS IN MALAYSIA

May 13, 1969 – that was the memorable day when racial violence broke out in Malaysia. We were caught unprepared and subjected to day and night curfews. Everyone was forced by law to stay in-doors or at home for many months.

Over the years, a great deal has been written of the racial riots that took place in Malaysia, beginning with the racial riots "explosion" on May 13, 1969. Following is an account of my personal experiences living through the many months of great turmoil and racial tension which resulted in many people of various races being killed, including Malays, Chinese and Indians. When it was finally over, we were thankful that our lives were safe and that we were spared any type of harm. At that time, my two young daughters were ages 3 and 2, and we were living in a small house in Petaling Jaya, a satellite township in the outskirts of Kuala Lumpur.

The whole episode was sparked off in the Malaysian capital of Kuala Lumpur and it quickly spread throughout Malaysia. On that fateful day, as I was driving home from work, I heard the announcement over the car radio, "Racial riots have broken out everywhere, and everyone is ordered to stay home! A state of emergency had been declared and the whole city is under 24-hour day and night curfew!"

In a state of panic, I managed to drive 15 miles safely home, only to find out via television reports that racial killing and fighting had broken out everywhere, especially in the predominantly Malays-controlled parts of the city. There was nothing we could do except to stay home and listen for news of the latest developments. Everything had come to a complete standstill and all shops and roads were closed, with hardly any traffic or business activity. The capitol city of Kuala Lumpur looked like a ghost town!

We were told that the native indigenous Malays were killing the Chinese and Indians, and destroying properties with fire and looting. There was widespread chaos everywhere, as violence and killing spread throughout the city. From our homes, we could hear the sounds of fire engines and ambulances rushing everywhere around the city. The pictures shown on the television depicted a war zone! It was as if a war had broken out and everyone was very nervous and apprehensive about things.

Though the media was not reporting an accurate picture of what was happening, mainly for political reasons, reports showed a lot of killing and fighting all over the capital. City police and security forces seemed helpless in dealing with the very serious civil uprising and fighting. There were even reports of Malay policemen hesitating to stop the violence where Malays were involved, and some even joined the rioters to fight the non-Malays. For many days, fierce fighting and widespread destruction were reported everywhere. In defense, the Chinese and Indians began to retaliate by joining forces to counter-attack the Malays thus causing even more bloodshed and destruction of property.

The endless riots escalated day after day and the continuing unrest eventually developed into a major crisis, causing a state of national emergency in Malaysia. The country was virtually ruled by marshal law. With the initial 24-hour curfew, everyone was confined to their homes and not allowed to get out of their homes, not even to get essential food, and if anyone were caught, they would be arrested and prosecuted! Offenders even ran the risk of being shot at by the police and security forces. We literally lived in fear of being injured or killed, or being harassed by the rioters who seemed to be everywhere, making it unsafe even to step out of the safety of our own home.

As we locked ourselves indoors, we occasionally heard screams of horror or crying, indicating that something terrible had happened, usually of people being brutally beaten or killed on the streets. Someone would shout a warning if rioters were sighted and warned to remain indoors or be killed or shot at. Just the sounds of the screaming and shouting sent chills down our spine! There were emergency and police vehicles rushing around to suppress the violence and to safeguard property even as many buildings were set on fire by the rioters.

Normal life for us had virtually come to a standstill. Trapped in the safety of our own homes, businesses were closed and all workers had to stay home. The "on again off again" daily curfew lasted at least three months. The hours of the daily curfew were slowly reduced each day as the intensity and frequency of the racial clashes slowly abated. Since we were unprepared for the long hours of curfew, we were forced to live on canned food and whatever we had in the pantry, which we soon grew bored of.

As the long and dreary days dragged on, our children began complaining, wanting to know why they had to stay in the house all the time and could not go out to play. "Why do we have to stay in the house all the time? We have nothing to do but eat, sleep and play. We want to go to the playground!" They were missing their neighbors and friends. They were also getting restless and wanted to go to the playground. Even the adults were getting restless and wondered how long the "lock in" was going to last, and when life was ever going to return to normal again.

Slowly, new laws were introduced as daily life and business barely returned to normal. Measures were taken in the hope of creating political stability in the country and to appease the indigenous Malays population. It was reported that the primary reason for the racial riots was that the native Malays were disenfranchised over the years and were tired of the setbacks they had suffered in every aspect of society, especially in their economic and social wellbeing.

Even though it is now a distant memory, the Malaysian riots of May 13, 1969 is still hotly and endlessly debated, and contradicted by the various factions of society. However, I am ever so thankful that my family and I survived the ordeal of the racial riots and that we were unharmed, though we were greatly inconvenienced.

CHAPTER 11
THE DIFFICULT ROAD TO SUCCESS

It is often said that the sure way to success in life is a good and solid education. When in school, our teachers were often heard saying, "If you expect to succeed in life, you must study hard and get good grades in order to find a job and live a successful life". How true that this statement has proven to be!

Securing a good education was a big challenge for my brothers, sisters, and me. It did not come easy for us, as we endeavored to survive the hardships and interruptions of World War II. Not only did the war years interrupt our primary and secondary education, it caused us to suffer a tremendous setback. Imagine missing 3 years of secondary school and having to "jump start" our studies again after the war was over!

For a few of my older siblings, the setback deprived them of the opportunity to complete their high school education and obtain the much sought-after Senior Cambridge Examination School Certificate, which is equivalent to the U.S. High School diploma. Most of us practically had to re-learn the English language as a result of not speaking or writing English for several years. To make matters worse, higher mathematics and other sciences were added to our learning. Studying these new subjects was like studying "Greek" to us! Everything was so foreign.

For me, the "difficult road to success" began with those difficult and uncertain post World War II years and the tough decisions I had to make while facing the uncertainties of my future. It was hard deciding whether to pursue higher studies by going to college, or to get out and find a suitable vocation. This also applied to my brother, Peter, and my sisters, Rebecca and Esther, who also faced a very uncertain future. Of necessity, I resorted to teaching the English language in a Chinese elementary school for a year. That one year's ordeal left me devastated and determined to find a way out and for me, that way out was to find a way to follow Rebecca to study in the U.S.A.

Success in my career did not come by easy either. Although I was blessed with a good engineering job in the United States soon after graduation, I was unknowingly made a victim of race discrimination. It was a terrible setback in my engineering career, which had barely just begun, and had crushed my hopes of a great engineering career. Rather than seek retribution, I decided to leave that lucrative job and return home to Singapore.

That disappointing episode, however, brought about even greater blessings the Lord had in store for me. As one would say, "whatever the devil meant it for evil, the Lord meant it for good!" and as Christian believers often would say, "When God closes one door, He always opens another door!" An even better door of opportunity was opened to me as God opened the door for me to a wonderfully new engineering career in Singapore and Malaysia that spanned over 20 years, covering various engineering fields!

Among my father's many favorite scripture versus are "Be of good courage, and he shall strengthen your heart, all ye that hope in the Lord;" (Psalm 31:24) and "We know that all things work together for good to them that love God, to them who are called according to His purpose (Romans 8:28). My father also traveled the "difficult road to success." I was touched by a very interesting story my father had once told us. When he was a young boy, his mother earned a small salary as a "traveling gospel reader" for early missionaries to China. To help his mother, he would go out to the woods to find any kind of odd job, including the very unpleasant job of collecting dog waste and selling it to the farmer for pennies.

As an adult, my father also faced the gigantic task of building the early Church in Singapore during very difficult economic times. For years, father would travel the streets of Singapore on a bicycle, rain or shine, for the sake of the church and his ministry. Thus he earned the reputation of being a "Bicycle Pastor" from the early missionaries to Singapore. During his visit to a Methodist church in Minnesota in 1948, when he mentioned that he was known as the "Bicycle Pastor" in Singapore, the church literally sent him a bicycle in the mail! The road to success for father was made even more difficult due to the fact that he earned very little as an itinerant preacher and pastor of a small church. The local church was too poor to afford him a decent salary, let alone provide sufficiently for his large and needy family.

When my father retired from active ministry in the church, he had no "roof over his head", so to speak. He and my mother lived on a very small Church pension even after serving the Methodist Church for over 30 years! However, they were blessed with children who loved and cared for them, and pulled their resources together to provide them with a lovely home in which to enjoy their retirement. My parents were very thankful for their many blessings in spite of the hardships they faced over the years. To Christian friends he met everywhere, my father was often heard expressing high praise for his children who cared enough to provide for their needs in order that they could enjoy a comfortable retirement life.

For my other siblings, the road to success was neither easy not without uncertainties either. Though everyone was blessed with a set of good genes and intellect, not everyone had the opportunity or the financial means to go overseas for higher studies. With the exception of Rebecca, Esther and I, who had scholarships to study in the U.S.A., Peter, Joseph and Benjamin had to go on "work study" programs at the universities in order to pay their way through college Even though they had some college subsidies, without financial assistance from home, they had to work part-time in order to meet their college expenses.

My older brother Peter's story was an exceptional one. The story of his "difficult road to success" included tremendous struggles against all odds, including his state of poor health. Difficult as it was, Peter not only worked several jobs in order to earn enough to support himself through college, he struggled hard to earn two degrees, a Bachelor of Science and a Master of Science, in spite of his handicaps and failing health which cut his life short at the age of 32.

CHAPTER 12
MY CAREER PATH: DRAMATIC CHANGES

In His divine plan and wisdom, God seemed to have ordained the direction of my life as well as the course of my engineering career as it saw dramatic changes.

Even as I finished high school, I faced my future with uncertainty and great apprehension. I had never thought of being a teacher and yet that was what I had to do in order to discipline myself and hopefully earn some money to help the family. After some trepidation, I realized that teaching was not "my cup of tea" and I desperately wanted to get out of it. With whatever little bit of money I had saved, my hope was to go overseas to study.

My big break miraculously came when God opened the door for me to go to college in America with my elder sister, Rebecca. In my freshman year at Puget Sound, when asked what I aspired to become, I did not have an answer. Being a rather short Asian boy, I sat up front in my mathematics class. My professor, Mr. Goman noticed that I was good at math. He suggested, "You should consider studying engineering since you are good at math." I had not heard of an engineer up to that point, but I took his suggestion.

My first great job was as an assistant engineer with a company in San Francisco. I saw a great future in front of me, as I designed dams. Upon returning to Singapore, I worked with Exxon Singapore in the petroleum industry, working on petroleum engineering projects and little of pure engineering work.

For the next 10 years, I found myself working for Exxon Malaysia, my job still involving many aspects of the petroleum industry but very little of engineering nature. Regardless, I made good progress in my career with Exxon and took on every task in stride, not realizing that my job would include such activities as marketing operations, plant operation, staff training and administrative management, but not engineering!

After the racial riots in Malaysia, I felt compelled to return to Singapore for my peace of mind and also for the sake of my children's education. My wife and I had decided that we wanted the children to get the best standard of education, which was to be found in Singapore.

Hence, my career changed direction again. I worked as Operations Manager for Skilled Engineering Pty. (Australia) for awhile, recruiting and placing technical personnel. Next I moved into the shipbuilding industry. From shipbuilding, it seemed like the natural thing to progress into marine engineering and construction, and I was blessed with an exciting and challenging career with McDermott South East Asia for the next 5 years.

During the time before my family emigrated from Singapore to the U.S.A. in 1983, my career took yet another turn, and I worked as Personnel and Administrative Manager for a Dutch engineering company in Singapore. Although I was working in an engineering environment, my responsibilities were mainly human resources and office management!

Just before my retirement in 1992, my career took a final dramatic change as I took on the position of Data Entry Operator with McMillan Publishing Inc. in Wilmette, Illinois. Since the beginning of my career until then, I found that life had taken me on a very dramatic detour from my engineering background up to this point!

CHAPTER 13
LIVING THE "GOOD" LIFE

My family was living the "good" life in Singapore when our children were very young. Being gainfully employed, we could afford to enjoy a reasonably "good" life.

While in America, we have often been asked by our American friends what life was like in Singapore, thinking that we were from Shanghai or China. Some people even asked us, "How was your life under the Communists in Singapore, or was it Shanghai? How did you learn to speak English? Isn't Singapore in China?" These and other questions seem to indicate just how little most Americans know about Singapore. When we were asked as to why we decided to leave such a great place, we would say, among other things, that we wanted our children to get a good education, and also to start a new life in America, the "land of milk and honey" (so we thought).

In Singapore, English was the main language taught in our mission-sponsored Christian schools, and Chinese was an optional subject, unless one chose to enter a Chinese language school. Even though my parents were from China, we did not study Chinese and the only Chinese language we had learned was to speak our mother tongue dialect, thus we were very ignorant of the Chinese language, strange as it may seem.

In his memoirs describing his nation-building achievements, the Senior Minister of Singapore, Mr. Lee Kuan Yew, the so-called "architect" of Singapore, said, "Singapore has progressed from 'Third World to the First' meaning that Singapore has become a great country and it has been rated the most modern city in Asia. It also has the highest standard of living in Asia. It was in such an affluent society that our children were blessed to have enjoyed a "good" life before we moved to the United States.

My wife, Doris, and I were financially able to afford a relatively comfortable standard of living and provided well for our children. We have been blessed with four godly young children whom we raised and nurtured in Singapore. My wife was a qualified dental nurse assigned to manage the Dental Clinic at the well-known Methodist Girls' School. She had a good dental job and I was blessed with a successful and challenging engineering career, having worked for over 30 years for several large American-owned companies, and earning a good income. As such, we had sufficient resources to provide adequately for our children's needs.

Relatively speaking, one could say that we lived a "good life" in Singapore as both of us had good earning power, at a time when we could even afford a full-time domestic help, also to help take care of our young children. Besides sufficient food, our children had fun things such as toys and nice clothing, some of which were found lacking in our own childhood days. Although the cost of living in Singapore was considered one of the highest in Asia, we could afford and enjoy such amenities as air-conditioning, considered a luxury in the tropical climate, washing machine, and fairly decent foodstuff. Once or twice weekly, especially during the weekend or holiday, we have the luxury of a nice meal at a restaurant or food court. We often enjoyed treats to a nice home-cooked meal at a relative's home and there were many!

Though we did not have the luxury of frequent travel out of Singapore, for the holidays, we did enjoy occasional road trips to the hilltop resorts in Malaysia. During our stay in Malaysia, we were able to enjoy occasional getaways to the hilltop resorts of Fraser's Hill, Cameron Highlands or the Genting Highlands. It was such a treat to get away from the tropical heat to enjoy the cool mountain air now and then. Our first major trip out of the country was when we left Singapore to migrate to America in 1983. A day out to the beach, or to the many tourist places such as the Jurong Bird Park or Sentosa Island, was always an exciting event for the children. After my frequent bowling sessions, the children often enjoyed a lunch treat to "dim sum", a favorite Chinese food.

Our children were blessed to be able to study at the highly acclaimed English stream Methodist Mission school. Our son had his elementary education at the Anglo-Chinese School, Singapore and our daughters at the Methodist Girls' School. Both these schools were known to have very high academic standards. Blessed with a good solid education in Singapore and Christian background, our children were well equipped to study in America and to look forward to live the "American Dream".

Having been brought up with a strong Christian foundation and sound Christian values, our children connected well with the local church family and the Christian community. Our social life was centered mostly on activities with relatives and fellow Christians. Events associated with Easter and Christmas were the most exciting and meaningful for our family. Every year, they looked forward to Christmas and the great parties hosted by the American companies that I worked for.

Our children always enjoyed participating in church musicals and kids' drama. They sang both at the school and church choirs. Putting together plays at home was something we were regularly treated to at Christmas. Our girls were taught to appreciate music from a very young age. They were taught to play the piano by their mother when they were young, and later had private piano lessons on a more advanced level.

We lived the "good" life in Singapore when there were

frequent family gatherings and celebrations, as we were blessed with many relatives and friends. Such events as birthdays and anniversaries were frequent occasions for the children to enjoy a good time, especially with other young children. The yearly Chinese Lunar New Year festivities brought much joy and fun for the children. Not only were there plenty of good food and delicious Chinese New Year snacks, the children were always showered with those delightful red "ang pows" (or little red envelopes filled with pocket money).

Between 1970 and 1983, we lived in four different homes in various parts of Singapore. Though not by choice, we did not live very long in each home. During those unsettling years, circumstances were such that caused us to move several times thus causing everyone considerable inconvenience and undue disruptions. However, by the grace of God, we were able to cope well with those unsettling years.

We owned our first house at the Faber Hills Housing Estate where we lived from 1970 to 1973. It was of a contemporary brick construction with a nice split-level living and dining room. We had a nice backyard where the children enjoyed playing in the outdoors. We enjoyed frequent visits from relatives and friends who came to visit our new home, that was especially exciting for our young children. At that time, we had two small Pekinese puppies which the children loved to play with. As we did not know how to properly care for them, we eventually had to give them away, and parting with our adorable pets was really a sad experience for the children.

When we lived at Faber Hills, our daughters, Debbie and Phoebe were ages 5 and 4 and our son, Timothy was just 2 years old and our daughter, Muriel, the little baby in the family. We had a full-time live-in housemaid to look after the children, to see to their needs, especially when their parents were at work. Faber Hills was quite a distance from the city, so we had decided to move closer to the city, also because the environment near the Estate was exposed to the highly polluted air from of the nearby industrial area. Then when my father went home to be with the Lord, leaving behind his widowed wife who seemed lonely, we lived with her for a season at the Winstedt Road apartment.

My mother was having health problems and suffered from her deteriorating diabetic condition for a number of years. Being unable to take care of herself, she had a full-time maid to look after her and she was glad to live with us. It was comforting for her to be close to her loved ones and to enjoy the company of our children, first at Winstedt Road, then later at our Saunders Road home. Sadly, my mother's diabetic condition deteriorated so badly that she eventually lost both of her legs and succumbed to the lingering diabetes in 1975.

Winstedt Road was at a convenient location, near to the famous tourist outdoor Newton food court. My wife continue to work at the School Dental Clinic on Mt. Sophia and. I commuted daily to work at the Jurong. We enjoyed a "good" life at our Winstedt Road home that was within walking distance to the Newton Food Court. We had occasional treats at the Newton Food Court when we wanted a savor the tasty "hawker-style" food. that was a nice change from the normal home-cooked meals.

From 1975 to 1983, we lived at 4-C Winstedt Road. Our three young girls were going to school at the Methodist Girls' School on Mount Sophia, the same school where their mother worked, and Timothy was going to the Anglo-Chinese School at Barker Road. Being busy working people, we had little time to properly care for our children before and after school. Thus they had learned to be somewhat independent at a young age as they took care of their own needs, with help from our hired maid.

Having my mother in our care, we then rented a 2-level home on Saunders Road, with more living area and the convenience of within walking distance to the children's Khee Fatt Kindergarten nearby. Our three younger children attended this kindergarten and we loved the convenience of being close to town and within close proximity to the busy Orchard Road tourist area, a great shopping center.

One of our children's most memorable childhood years were spent at the Khee Fatt Kindergarten located near to our Saunders Road home, just 50 yards away. Phoebe was the first to enter, followed by Timothy and finally Muriel. They were thrilled to be taught basic kindergarten lessons including some Chinese language, and they also enjoyed doing fun things such as handicrafts and performing in kids' concerts. It was a joy to see them walk to the kindergarten in the company of our hired maid and especially to see them dressed in smart looking uniforms, with fond memories to cherish.

Such was the "good" life we lived in Singapore as we watched our children growing up. As little children, our three younger children grew up with many exciting experiences during their impressionable ages. Their kindergarten days at the Khee Fatt Kindergarten were filled with new and exciting experiences, not just learning both English and Chinese, but also getting a taste of what it was like on stage with taking part in children's drama and musical events. For a short season, my mother stayed with her full time nursing maid, close to my family in a room on the lower level of our house

When my mother went home to be with the Lord, we were able to own our own home at Jalan Merlimau, off Thomson Road, also near the city. It had a nice front yard where the children played and where we entertained friends. It was a nice 2-level single- family house that had a large front yard and even a mature papaya tree that bore sweet papayas. The small back yard provided a needed utility area and a few banana trees as well. A paid Indian gardener maintained our garden for a small fee. There were plenty of things for the children to enjoy and do fun things for their own entertainment. We felt that we were really living the "good" life in Singapore. Unfortunately, we were compelled to move away a few years later, due to a couple of bad and unruly neighbors!

Up until the time when we emigrated from Singapore in 1983, we lived in another Winstedt Road apartment. Our girls were attending the Methodist Girls' School in Mount Sophia where Doris worked, and Timothy was going to the Anglo-Chinese School at Barker Road. Being busy working folks, we had inadequate quality time for our children before and after school. Needless to say, they learned independence at a young age and they did a marvelous job of taking care of their own needs, with some help from a hired help maid. Our two older girls did well to look after their younger siblings when they were like "home alone" kids with very busy working parents.

Although we were not considered wealthy, we were blessed with the means to provide adequately for the family while enjoying the "good" life in Singapore during the children's childhood. We had an abundance of good food, nice clothing, and living in the comfort of our home, and spending quality time with relatives and friends at numerous family gatherings. Needless to say, with many church and school events, our children led a very eventful life in Singapore. These are just a sampling of our children's teenage impressionable years living the "good" life in the country of their birth, that is, the bustling, modern and exotic tropical country of the Republic of Singapore.

OUR CHILDREN: THE WONDERFUL YEARS
LIVING THE "GOOD" LIFE

*1980 (left to right: Doris, Phoebe,
Muriel, Debbie, Tim)*

*Taken at our Winsteadt Road home –
1980 (left to right: Doris, Phoeb,
Muriel, Debbie, Tim)*

Family Portrait 2005

Our Jalan Merlimau home, Singapore – 1975

Family Portrait with Pual Jr., Doris & children – 1979
(left to right: Muriel, Phoebe, Debbie, Tim)

CHAPTER 14
OFF WE GO!...TO THE U.S.A.!

Our American friends often asked us questions such as, *"Why did you all leave Singapore? Did you not enjoy a good life in such a nice country as Singapore?*

On July 13, 1983, a new chapter of our lives began when we landed in America, and the course of our lives changed dramatically. The long-awaited day had finally arrived as we prepared to board the Japanese Airlines jet airplane that would take us to the "land of great opportunity" – the United States of America! It was such a significant day because we had waited five long years to see our dreams finally fulfilled, the amount of time it took for us to obtain our legal papers to become legal immigrants.

In retrospect, the idea of migrating to the United States perhaps took root from those years' when I was studying in America. In fact, thoughts of those seven wonderful years haunted me during those 24 years I was back in Singapore. Having had the opportunity to experience the American way of life, I often related my experiences to my children. In response, they would ask, "You always tell us of your wonderful years in America. What was it really like? When can you bring us there? Can we go there to live and study as well?"

For a while, even though I never pursued it actively, the idea of relocating my family to American remained at the back of my mind. In the late 1970s, the oil crisis had affected various industries in Singapore, and my career in the petroleum, shipbuilding and marine engineering industries appeared unstable. After much prayer seeking the Lord's will, and with support from my family, I decided to take the first step to apply for U.S. immigrant papers.

"There has to be a breakthrough", I thought to myself, "not only for the sake of my career but also for the sake of my children's education and future." Our prayers were answered toward the end of 1982.We received a call from the American Embassy in Singapore, informing us that our immigrant status application had been approved and that our next step was to go through a "screening" and a medical checkup. Our children were overjoyed and from then on, would constantly ask, "When can we go to America? We need to pack and make plans for the big move soon!"

With all the papers in place, the date was set for our departure. Prior to that, our days were spent attending the many farewell parties and family gatherings, on top of making preparations for the big move! Not only did we have to decide what things to bring and what to dispose off, there was a long shopping list of things that could not be found in the States. We had to make sure that electrical items were of the correct voltage if we were to bring them with. What we could not bring, we either sold them at a garage sale or gave away to friends and family. In the midst of the confusion, we suddenly realized that we had almost sold off our valuable wedding present at a ridiculously low price, that of our precious upright piano!

Our children were getting anxious for the momentous day, and for several days prior to our departure, convinced us to drive them to the airport to experience what it would be like on that "big day". Being young and innocent children, they were simply thrilled to enjoy the "make believe" experience, of going to the airport and pretending that we were preparing to board a plane to depart to America!

July 13, 1983 finally arrived, the big day of our departure. It was both a happy and bitter sweet day. On the one hand, everyone was very excited about embarking on a new adventure to this new country called America! However, we were also to leave behind everything that we were accustomed to, including all of our many friends and loved ones. There were lots of hugs to go around and some were visibly in tears as we bade goodbye to everyone and saying, "all the best to everyone and to Singapore!"

As our airplane took off from the Singapore Changi Airport runway, some of us fought back tears while others remained in deep thought, anticipating what it would be like to live in a foreign country that they had never seen before, except in some pictures in magazines and on television. For the next 20 hours, we flew over the South China Sea and the Pacific Ocean, then made an overnight stopover in Tokyo, Japan, and finally landed in Los Angeles, California. Everyone breathed a sigh of relief when the aircraft touched down in Los Angeles. We felt exhausted after the long flight, perhaps suffering from jet lag as well, but so very thrilled and excited that we had finally reached America!

Completely tired and disorientated, we waited in long lines at the U.S. Immigration and U.S. Customs checkpoints, and were screened by the U.S. Customs. We had made plans to stay in Los Angeles to rest and recuperate before continuing to our final destination in Houston, Texas. However, our hosts, the Berwicks family had other ideas. "Now that you are in Los Angeles, we must show you some of the sights, including the world famous Hollywood Studios. You can't come all the way to America and not visit Disneyland! You will thoroughly enjoy the fun and excitement of this world famous great amusement park!"

Before coming to America, we had heard of the so-called "culture shock" that others had experienced when they first came, either as U.S. immigrants or as a casual visitor. We felt somewhat relieved that this was not the case with us. Looking back, we were blessed to have been introduced to the Berwicks family in Los Angeles. We were truly thankful for their kindness and warm hospitality, as they extended a very warm and friendly reception to us. What a nice beginning for our "Adventures - as "New Immigrants to the U.S.A.!" we surmised.

CHAPTER 15
OUR ADVENTURES IN THE U.S.A.
PART I – AS "FOREIGN STUDENTS"

*A*s young children, we used to hear my father say, *"America is like heaven on earth!"* So we would dream about going to America – even as a 'foreign student'.

"America is beautiful and wonderful. It is like 'heaven on earth!'" Those were my father's impressions when he returned from Boston in 1948, after attending the General Conference of the Methodist Church. He was the first elected Asian delegate to attend this world conference. As he told us how wonderful America was, we could only dream of going there ourselves – even if only as a foreign student.

Of course, we did not have the financial means to make that happen. Whenever we brought up the subject, my father would pose the question, "Where will we find the means to finance your college education in America, not to mention the cost of traveling to such a faraway place?" We realized that the only way we could make it to America was to secure a scholarship or find someone who can help us financially. "It will not be easy to send even just one of you to America, let alone so many of you!" he added. "Are you sure that you will be able to survive so far away from home?" With those questions in mind and no easy answers available, we could only pray for a miracle to happen.

That miracle happened when our kind and generous uncle, Uncle Khoo, provided my sister and me with 2 tickets on the ocean freighter to America. His trading business was flourishing and he decided to share his blessings with us. In addition, God provided both academic and financial scholarships for my sister Rebecca, my brother Peter and I. Through the efforts of my father's missionary friends, Dr. & Mrs. Paul B. Means, the Wesleyan Guilds of Oregon provided a full music scholarship for Rebecca to study music at Wilamette University in Oregon. Another of father's missionary friend, Dr. M. Dodsworth, found an old college roommate, John E. Love, to sponsor my college education. Peter found his way via London to Baldwin-Wallace College in Ohio, where he obtained a work-study program to finance his college education. Needless to say, we were truly blessed by the financial generosity of all these people so we could study in America. In a sense, we felt like "early pioneers", leaving home for a faraway country to study.

We were considered foreign or international students, coming from another country. We not only faced the challenge of trying to overcome the "culture shock" of trying to live and adjust to a new way of life in a strange new place, we also faced the challenge of trying to adapt to the climate, which was very different from the tropical climate of Singapore. Even with scholarships, we needed to work part-time to earn some pocket money, not expecting money from home even if we needed help. Our college years were filled with many interesting experiences and challenges, notwithstanding the fact that we were very far away from home, and not knowing as to when we might finish our studies and head on home.

OUR ADVENTURES IN THE U.S.A. AS FOREIGN STUDENTS

Paul Jr.'s at Soldiers' Field, Chicago, Illinois – 1952

Cross-country train ride from Chicago to Seattle - 1952

Paul as a Freshman at College of Puget Sound, in Tacoma, Wash. – 1952

Rebecca & friend Lily Ho on board the S.S. "Steel Chemist"

Taken in our new home in Tulsa. (Tim, Phoebe, Debbie, Muriel) – 1986

Rebecca & Paul Jr. visiting the Lincoln Memorial in Wash. DC – 1952

Muriel plays the French Horn in High School - 1985

CHAPTER 16
OUR ADVENTURES IN THE U.S.A
PART II – AS NEW IMMIGRANTS

As new immigrants in the United States of America, we faced many challenges, including adjusting to the change from the hot and humid tropical climate of Singapore to that of the temperate climate. However, the relatively warm weather in Houston, Texas was easy for us to adapt to. Once we were comfortably settled in our home, one of our first concerns was to find suitable employment, as well as make plans for the children's education. "We are finally living the American way of life!" so we thought to ourselves.

We had chosen to settle down in Houston, Texas because that was where my brother, Joseph, and his family lived and where he ran his own business. Thinking that Texas was in the oil belt, I had high hopes of finding work relative to my engineering experience. Alas, I was disillusioned and found out that the oil crisis in the United States has affected us back in Singapore. Subsequently, I was able to help with Joseph's printing business, which helped provide income for our daily living.

Soon after we moved into our apartment, our eldest daughter, Debbie, began getting anxious about going to college at Oral Roberts University in Tulsa, Oklahoma. In the midst of preparing for our first hurricane, Hurricane Alicia, we frantically tried to make arrangements to send her to Tulsa with the Fall term soon to begin. As we sent her off to Tulsa, we breathed a sigh of relief. However, a sense of sadness overcame us, realizing that we had sent our first child away from home! We took comfort, though, knowing that she would be home for the Thanksgiving and Christmas holidays.

We were very happy when the opportunity opened for Debbie to go to college; that might not otherwise have been the case back in Singapore. For one thing, not everyone had the opportunity in Singapore to attend college, only those with exceptionally high grades and those with strong financial means. Having considered all the factors, we thought to ourselves, "Why should we not take advantage of the opportunity to migrate to America? By doing so, it would also open the door for our other children to further their studies."

Our initial experiences as new immigrants were not without many uncertainties and anxieties. Unable to secure a good, stable job, we continually had to look to God for strength and help. When Phoebe joined Debbie at Oral Roberts University, we decided to relocate there in 1985, after which things got even worse. I decided to invest in a business, which resulted in my painful financial loss when it failed. Despite that, God, in His mercy and grace, opened the door for a new employment opportunity in Chicago, where my brother, Ben, and family lived. With Ben and his friend's help, I found work at McMillan Publishing Inc, together with my wife and daughter. That changed the course of our lives as new immigrants from then on. Thus with our faith and trust in our loving, merciful Father, our life changed much for the better and we were finally blessed with a good life!

OUR ADVENTURES IN THE U.S.A. AS NEW IMMIGRANTS

Taken in our new home in Tulsa (Tim, Phoebe, Debbie, Muriel) - 1986

Enroute to U.S.A. at Narita Airport, Japan

Our four children
(left to right: Timothy, Muriel, Phoebe & Debbie) - 1988

Our Family Portrait with John, Keith & Alan & grand kids – 1995

New U.S. Immigrants welcome Singapore – friend Sie Chin Hong to our Tulsa home – 1986

At our first home in Webster, Texas (left to right: Debbie, Doris, Muriel, Phoebe & Tim) – 1983

CHAPTER 17
A RUDE AWAKENING!

*A*s *new immigrants, we were greeted by hurricane "Alicia", as it hit the Texas coast in July 1983, right after we first arrived in America. For us, it was a "rude awakening".*

After arriving in Houston, Texas, we were finally settled in our apartment when we were told that hurricane Alicia was approaching Texas! It was described as a category "3" hurricane and could cause immense damage and possibly loss of lives. We had less than 2 days to get ready to face this hurricane. We were told to stock up food to last a few days, as well as have plenty of batteries and candles on hand.

With the constant warning on the television and on the radio, we braced ourselves for the onslaught of the impending hurricane that was our first experience of such a storm! "What a nice welcome for us!" we thought to ourselves. "We could have not chosen a worse time to move here" Everything was so unsettled and we were just trying to get adjusted to living in a strange new place, and we felt the hot Texas summer heat so exhausting although not as humid as it was in Singapore. In addition to dealing with "culture shock", we found ourselves in the midst of a powerful hurricane that was poised to hit the

Texas coast and the "eye" of the hurricane was projected right over our area!

We were literally "living out of our suitcases" while making preparations for the hurricane. We were still finding our way around in the area, as we drove around in a borrowed car to purchase essential items. Although mindful of the impending hurricane, we were still excited about exploring our way around town and looking forward to living the American way of life that we had heard so much about.

With everything in place, we huddled together in our 2-room apartment, sleeping on the kitchen floor, which was the safest room, away from the glass windows. As we listened to news broadcasts on the radio, we were really frightened. We had never experienced a hurricane and did not really know what to expect! We told the children, "We must stay calm and pray for God to protect us and keep us safe!" While strong winds blew outside and the heavy rains came down, we could see objects and roof shingles flying as we looked out the living room windows

We soon heard on the radio that hurricane Alicia had made landfall at Galveston, Texas and was heading its way towards us in Houston! Galveston and Texas City had both been evacuated. We were expecting the "calm before the storm" when we heard a sudden calmness in the air as the eye of the hurricane passed over us. It lasted nearly 15 minutes, followed by more rain and strong winds.

The biggest question on everyone's mind at that moment was, "Is the storm over yet? Are we out of danger yet?" Anxious, all we could do was stay calm and watch the latest satellite pictures of the storm and the many fallen trees and all the damage it had caused. For us, it was indeed a "rude awakening" by hurricane Alicia. Even at such a time of fear and anxiety, we felt God's abiding peace! Thank God that we were safe!

CHAPTER 18
ROAMING "NOMADS"

Circumstances were such that, as new immigrants, we found ourselves in a "state of flux" so to speak, moving first from Texas to Oklahoma, then to Chicago – all in a matter of 3 years! That was the way things turned out for us, though not of our own choice.

Never in our wildest dreams could we have imagined that we would move from one state to another in our first few years as new immigrants to the United States of America. Being unable to find suitable employment in Houston, I suggested to my wife and family, "Why don't we move to Tulsa so that we can be closer to Debbie and Phoebe at O.R.U.? For one thing, we can get away from the Texas heat and second of all, our girls can live at home while going to college and thus help them save on living expenses"

In Tulsa, we rented a single family home near the campus of Oral Roberts University. Our two other children, Timothy and Muriel, were in high school at that time. We got to know quite a number of international students, including Singapore students, and we hosted numerous events at our home. We were also involved in a church there, Christian Chapel Church, and were blessed with the fellowship we found among our "spiritual" brothers and sisters.

Our home was constantly filled with activity, as students dined with us frequently, and church friends often visited us. Still unable to obtain decent employment, I decided to go into business with a Christian, however, the business that I invested failed miserably. It was then that God opened up the opportunity for me to work for McMillan Publishing Inc. in Chicago. Hence, in 1988, I moved to Chicago and my wife Doris, Timothy and Muriel remained in Tulsa, while both of them finished high school there.

Upon graduation, Debbie was offered a position with Baxter Pharmaceuticals in Chicago, and Phoebe was able to find a job at McMillan Publishing also. With the three of us in Chicago, we went through two unsettling years, traveling between Tulsa and Chicago whenever we had an extended weekend or holiday.

For the first time since moving to the United States, I found myself with a secure job at McMillan Publishing Inc. Once Timothy and Muriel were done with school, I suggested to Doris, "Why don't you all join us in Chicago so that our family can be together again. McMillan has a number of job openings and you might be able to find a job here as well" So as it turned out, three of our family members ended up working for McMillan in the Company's different divisions. Timothy chose to attend the University of Illinois in Chicago, and Muriel went to Wheaton College. God had once again, by His divine intervention, opened the door for all three of us to work for the same company and the family to be together again!

In 1989, after living in the United States for 5 years, we were finally able to own our first home in Skokie, Illinois. Although it was nice to have everyone living under the same roof again, we realized that it wouldn't be long before our children would go their own separate ways. That November, our daughter Debbie married her husband, John Harms and they move moved to Virginia where John had found employment as a Research Scientist and Debbie became a legal secretary in a large legal office.

As our future appeared less uncertain, we were able to plug ourselves into a spirit-filled church, something that we badly needed. Unexpectedly, in 1990, McMillan Publishing moved away to New Jersey and I found myself once again being unemployed. That was when we decided to move to Roselle, Illinois, a suburb of Chicago. Thus necessitating another big move! The move was financially advantageous to us because, for the first time, we found ourselves owning a home free of mortgage! By this time, I decided that it was time for me to retire.

Our final move came in 2001 as we found ourselves on the move one more time to Streetsboro, Ohio. Our second daughter, Phoebe, had married a minister, Rev. Alan Fung, and they were starting a church in Cleveland, Ohio. Since I was retired, Doris and I felt the call to support our son-in-law in his international ministry. God again blessed us financially with that move from Roselle, Illinois to Ohio!

We were again able to own our cozy home free of mortgage, a brand new condominium in the new township of Streetsboro, a suburb of Cleveland some 30 miles to the southeast of the city. At long last, we are happily settled in our permanent home and not feel like "roaming nomads" anymore!

CHAPTER 19
"MOTHERLY" SISTER

*A*t times she behaves and acts like a 'motherly' sister to all of us, one who really loves and cares for the family and her siblings, as it was perceived by her younger brothers and sisters. Even close family friends sometimes used to make remarks to this effect.

In a large family such as ours, the burden of caring and nurturing our younger siblings, especially during our childhood years, was a very demanding task. "One wonders how a mother could possibly have managed to attend to the needs of twelve children, It is wonderful that Ruth cared enough to play a "motherly" role sometimes, as our close family friends often commented.

During the time when I was young, housemaids were hard to come by, for us, that is, and not easily affordable. As such, my mother had to rely on the older children to share with the responsibilities of parenting, as well as helping with the household chores. The older children were often asked to help the younger ones in their studies and personal needs, such as getting dressed properly, eating proper meals and even personal hygiene!

Somehow, her "motherly role" was not only played out in our

early days, she seemingly continued to act this way even into her adult life. She has been blessed with financial independence, more so than some of her other siblings. By her nature, she cared enough to want to share her means with the needy

"Just like Mary and Peter, Ruth was deprived of the opportunity to earn the Senior School Certificate (equivalent of a high school diploma) because of the World War II disruptions, after having missed school for several years," father used to tell us. Despite this setback, she had a successful career as a qualified nurse, working hard for many years before her retirement. Even during her retirement, she continued to work at the Singapore Cheshire Home, reaching out to the physically handicapped.

Throughout her life, Ruth has deeply devoted herself to my family, caring for her younger siblings and nursing the sick. She even reaches out to her Christian friends from the church. She is ever willing and ready to give a helping hand to those who need nursing care or advice. She is ever ready to render her "motherly" concern, thus making use of her many years' nursing experience, whether it be at home or at the hospital.

My parents did well to instill in Ruth a deep sense of caring and concern for the young. Being single most of her life, Ruth is blessed with the means to give a helping hand to those in need, especially her siblings. She did not have much growing up, so her sense of value is such that, for one who does not know her well she might be thoughts of being overly thrifty. Food was very scarce when she was young, so to her, "Throwing away any edible food is just unthinkable and must be frowned upon!" Regardless, she deserves much credit for her "motherly": love and concern for her siblings. Somehow, such caring spirit seems to be not uncommon in many Asian families.

CHAPTER 20
"SELFLESS" PETER

*P*eter was a 'selfless' brother whose life was sadly cut short. Yet he had made a deep impact on everyone, his family and many friends. He was truly a remarkable brother!

To those who knew him well, especially the older siblings, Peter was a person of great compassion and he loved his family deeply. Thus we would call him our "selfless" brother. The oldest of six boys in my family, Peter had lived a godly and Christ-like life, only to succumb to cancer at the young age of 32 in 1961.He was at the prime of life, so to speak, with a good future for his career when he went home to be with the Lord. .

To me, Peter was "one of a kind", a person of sterling character and full of love, whose short life had touched many people. He was a man of great courage and strong determination to make his life count. Not without struggles, he was able to reach academic heights, but at a huge personal sacrifice. In-spite of being severely handicapped, physically and educationally, and not being able to complete his high school Peter managed to earn 2 degrees, a Bachelor of Science and a Master of Science.

"As a teenager, Peter was deprived of a high school diploma, due to his earlier battle with cancer, but he struggled against great odds to achieve his high academic goals," according to my parents. He joined my older sister, Mary, who was undergoing nursing training, in the U.K., hoping to find his way to go to college. Instead, he found himself hospitalized for a major surgery to remove part of his stomach due to a seriously bleeding ulcer. Soon after recuperating, Peter found his way to the United States, and enrolled at the Baldwin-Wallace College, thus fulfilling his dream of going to college in America. He made something remarkable of his life that deeply touched many lives.

Peter left Baldwin-Wallace College, in Berea, Ohio, in 1954 to join me at Oregon State College so that he could be closer, to my sister, Rebecca when she was at Wilamette University in Salem, Oregon and I was studying Oregon State University in Corvallis, Oregon. "We shared an apartment and thus were able to help each other financially" Being as thrifty and hard working as he was, Peter worked two part-time jobs while in college, literally 'burning the midnight oil', to complete his studies. Even so, he earned two degrees while struggling financially and with his health problem,

Peter was a greatly admired young man whose unconditional love touched many. He was completely devoted to helping his parents and siblings to the point of making deep personal sacrifices. Being the eldest, he always seemed very protective of his younger siblings. The old saying, "The good seem to die young" seem to aptly apply to my dear brother Peter. When he died on a warm June day in 1961, his parents and all of his siblings were at his bedside. The trauma of witnessing for the first time the passing of a loved one was just unbearable! In the last moments of Peter's life, I was so emotionally affected that my legs became partially paralyzed. That caused even more pain and sorrow to everyone. At his "home-going" celebration of life and funeral, many were heard to say, "What a great loss to see such a godly, wonderful and well-educated young man!"

CHAPTER 21
A "SAINTLY" SISTER

My sister Rebecca and I completed our Senior Cambridge Examinations - the equivalent of the U.S. High School Diploma) in the same year, which was 1951, and from there went on to college in America. We were blessed with good scholarships and the opportunity of experiencing college life in the United States of America.

My family was very proud of our sweet and talented sister, Rebecca, who was the fourth child. Born on February 27, 1931, Rebecca's life spanned 68 years of great success and achievements in her musical career, as well as her roles of wife and mother. We truly admire her devotion to serve God and His Church. As relayed by one of Rebecca's daughters, "Mom has accomplished what she was here for and she has done what she wanted to do."

In a tribute to her mother, she quotes the Bible saying, "Her children arise up and call her blessed, her husband also, and he praises her." Rebecca's high school alumni magazine wrote, "She did everything in a calm and un-harassed manner. None of us realized the amount of work she had put in till she was down with a stroke! Even then she did her best to find substitutes and rearrange schedules so that life could go on uninterrupted for others."

A long-time close friend of Rebecca's, school principal, Mrs. Elice Handy said, "Growing up with twelve siblings probably made her familiar with the role of a mediator when approached. As a young lady in school and, even in her adult years, she was a quiet and well-behaved girl who readily took on an assignment given to her, especially as a school or church organist." "Rebecca was unquestionably the most dedicated and committed musician for any occasion," her pastor was quick to add.

After graduating from Wilamette University in Oregon with a Bachelor of Science honors degree, she married her life mate, Dr. Wong Kong Meng, who had courted her for quite a few years, trying to win over her heart! Both led a wonderful life together, devoting their lives in service to the Church and to the community. Rebecca served God and her church through her musical talents, and Kong Meng served those around him with the God-given medical skills he was blessed with.

They were very devoted parents, as they raised and nurtured their two daughters, Carolyn and Florence, and two sons, Alan and Andrew. In their older years, they have enjoyed the deep love and accomplishments of their children, as well as their seven grandchildren, who all live in Australia with them.

"They loved to travel and see the world!" said their children. They were greatly blessed to be able to do just that during their retirement years, in addition to being doting grandparents to their adorable grandchildren.

Rebecca's selfless devotion to the music ministry in church, whether in Singapore, Malaysia or Australia, deserves recognition and high praise. She was very faithful in her role as pianist and organist for our father's Hinghwa Methodist Church in Singapore for many years. Talented and gifted, she was known for being a hardworking, reputable music teacher as well. In her own quiet and gentle way, Rebecca always served the church in a humble manner, and cared deeply for her family and friends, especially the needy.

Our younger sister, Esther, once said to her, "I treasure many precious, happy days with you growing up in our Sam Leong Road home in Singapore. Being a few years older than I, naturally you did the heavier, more physical chores to help mother in cooking, washing and ironing, etc. I am grateful for your many contributions to the family! You have always been a hard worker! Considering how little we had while growing up, we were never deprived of God's love, care and rich blessings upon us."

Indeed the words of the lovely song, "In His time... In His time... He makes something beautiful in His time" describe beautifully the life and nature of our dear beloved sister, mother and grandmother, Rebecca, for truly God had made something beautiful and marvelous when He brought Rebecca into this world. Her precious and inspiring life was tragically taken away from us on that sad day, December 17, 1999, in Adelaide, Australia, when she was unexpectedly called home to be with the Lord at the age of 68 after a very brief illness with her loved ones at her bedside.

As her brother, I would describe Rebecca as a "saintly" sister, and an endearing wife, mother and grandmother to her family in Australia and around the world. In leaving this earthly life so very suddenly and unexpectedly, Rebecca has left a void in the hearts and lives of her many loved ones, including her brothers and sisters.

Indeed we can all say, "The emptiness that we feel in our hearts with her demise will last until eternity when we shall be with her in heaven where she now rests in peace." I can honestly say of my dear sister that she had lived a wonderfully glorious and fulfilling life. God had truly made her an instrument of His love as she devoted her life to serving Christ and His Church, both in Singapore and in Australia.

In Loving Memory of
Rebecca HANG Deh Hua
27 February 1931 - 17 December 1999

Hang Deh Hua from the Class of 1951 is best remembered as being responsible for harmonising our School Song. Deh Hua's musical talent was evident since her school days. In 1950, she wrote a prize-winning song entitled "At the Break of Morn" when she was in Standard VIII. The 1950-51 school magazine reports:

Prize Winner

We are proud of Hang Deh Hua, who won a song competition sponsored by Radio Malaya ... Deh Hua has been in this school since Primary 1 and is pianist of the Wesley M.Y.F. and the Hinghwa Church.

After a brief illness, Hang Deh Hua passed away on 17 December 1999 at the age of 68 in South Australia. Her classmate and close friend, Mrs Moses Yu, paid this tribute to her:

~ *Deh Hua and I were Standard 3 classmates right after the war. She was a quiet, well-behaved girl who readily took on the role of mediator when approached ... growing up with twelve siblings probably made her familiar with the role.*

Deh Hua was the accompanist at our singing lessons (2 periods a week) and pianist at every school function. We sang songs like "My Heart Ever Faithful" and "The Trout" and Deh accompanied us with aplomb, never showing an accompanist's impatience or irritation.

In all the years I knew her, I've never known Deh Hua to get angry. I only heard of her getting upset and crying once - and this from a Malacca boy (he later became her husband!).

When Deh went to the US for further studies, she never failed to write at Christmas or remember birthdays. After she married in 1958, Deh devoted her time to church work. She played for numerous weddings and church functions. She had a great network of family

and friends and was always there with a listening ear for those who needed her, giving good advice and never divulging what she heard to others. She enthusiastically organised informal gatherings at her home but was never too busy to run an errand or help out in time of need.

Most of all, she did everything in a calm and unharassed manner. None of us realised the amount of work she put in till she was struck down with a stroke. Even then she did her best to find substitutes and rearrange schedules so that life could go on uninterrupted for others.

Deh Hua loved travelling. After recovering from a knee operation, she and her husband visited the Great Wall of China. They also toured Spain and Portugal and she was full of plans to go to England when she died.

In her daughter's words, "Mom has accomplished what she was here for and she has done what she wanted to do."

Truly as the Good Book says, "Her children arise up and call her blessed; her husband also, and he praiseth her." ~

Christmas Concert 1949 in school with Deh Hua in front row far right (top left); at the piano in her younger days (bottom left) and her Prize Winning Song (above)

CHAPTER 22
JOHN, THE "TALLEST"

The tallest of the six brothers, John was described as the "easy-going" one by his siblings. He lived a good life even though he left us at the early age of 46.

My father once commented that John would be the next preacher in our family, little did he know that John was called to serve God but did not have the opportunity to serve a church full-time and be another one to take after father's footsteps, besides our youngest brother, Benjamin. John felt led to the ministry, and then went on to Trinity Theological College in Singapore where he completed his theological studies. "He really struggled to find meaning for his life," as one would say.

By nature, John was often jokingly mentioned as "easy-going" by his other siblings, perhaps because of his good nature and unassuming personality. My mother used to say, "You are always hungry but you must also think of others in the family when food supply is not plentiful" Perhaps that was the reason that John grew to be the tallest, we all surmised. As a result, he was often asked to reach for things that were too high for anyone else to reach. His son, Martin, has also been blessed with his height and good looks. His siblings used to say to him, "John, you are always the nice guy, always trying to help others, that's why you got into unnecessary trouble now and then" But John was a person of integrity and a strong desire for his purpose-driven life, as I had perceived.

John was a very devoted brother, a lot of fun to be around and contributed much joy to the Hang family. He loved to laugh and had a good sense of humor, and able to relieve some of the stress and anxiety in stressful times. Always easy-going, he loved to play and have fun with his brothers and friends. His older siblings often had to remind him to stop playing and help them with the cleaning around the church! No matter how hard he tried to do his part, he would get distracted time and time again. It was his fun-loving personality that attracted his friends.

John had many talents, although he did not have the opportunity to go to college. According to my father, "John was deprived of an opportunity to pursue a college education in America as his other siblings, as well as the lack of financial resources at a time when we were needy. But he did finish his Senior Cambridge and went on to Trinity Theological College and did very well." Yet he had many hidden talents and abilities worthy of recognition. John had a good insurance career while serving part time in the Church and in Christian ministry. John and his wife, Irene, have raised three well-mannered and godly children, Martin, Alvin and Karen. He was a very devoted father and he cared deeply for his wife and family.

The "fruits of his labors" are evident in his remarkable family, one that brings honor to John and gives glory to God. John battled with liver cancer and was called home to be with the Lord after a brief illness. His children have done well in their lives, even after losing their father at a very young age. With the loving care of their mother, Irene, they have been blessed with remarkable achievements and successful careers.

CHAPTER 23
REMEMBERING DAVID

O*ne of the six younger boys in our family, David was nicknamed one of the "three musketeers"*

David was the fourth boy, the tenth child in the family, born in 1942 at the time when the Japanese warplanes were "raining" bombs all over Singapore. While everyone was running for their lives and seeking shelter from enemy bombs, my mother was giving birth to David. It was a terrifying ordeal for my poor mother! As my mother recalled, "I was terrified and visibly shaken, not knowing what was going to happen when David was born. Your father had to take all the children to the underground shelter beside the church compound. We were really blessed to stay alive!"

As a young boy, David and our two younger brothers, Joseph and Benjamin, were always very active and always hungry, considered somewhat "restless little boys". According to my mother, "I tried to discipline them and when they disobeyed, I would jokingly nickname them as, "the three musketeers" meaning the "restless ones".

David was a man with great desire and ambition. He also had great confidence in himself and in what he wanted to achieve in life. I considered him as someone blessed with a better than average IQ and somewhat of a "high achiever". Thus, I thought to myself, "David is very intelligent and gets good grades in school. We should find a way to help finance his university education, maybe even in Australia." So, together with my parents, we pulled our resources together to send him to Melbourne, Australia. There, David studied chemical engineering and proved himself worthy of his family's support.

With the family's financial support, as well as the moral support of my sister, Sarah, who was in Australia at that time, David graduated from the University of Melbourne. Afterwards, I was thrilled that David could join me in working for Exxon Malaysia, he in the Port Dickson refinery. Needless to say, I was very proud of my younger brother working in the same company as I was. He then married Susan Ong in a grand "double ring" wedding ceremony in Seremban, Malaysia.

David gained considerable experience in his coveted chemical engineering field. When the opportunity came his way, he made the ultimate move to leave Exxon and establish his own business, Sunlit Engineering Ltd. in Singapore. His business flourished and his business being successful, he and his family were blessed with a comfortable home.

Just when David found his life to be complete and fulfilling, he suddenly found himself the victim of cancer. That happened not long after we had just lost my brother, John. As we saw David struggle for his life, it seemed really sad that his whole world seemed to have been turned upside down. Despite his and short fruitful life, David had lived a godly and rewarding life till the age of 56 when he went home to be with the Lord As the endearing husband and father, David had left lasting legacy to his wife and children, as they seek comfort in the Lord as he is at rest eternally in heaven with God.

CHAPTER 24
AFTER FATHER'S FOOTSTEPS

The youngest of the children, Benjamin was thought to follow after his father's footsteps, by virtue of his nature and his talents, according to my parents.

It was 1944 and he Japanese forces were in control of Singapore when my mother gave birth to my parents' twelfth child, Benjamin. According to my father, "Mother had a very difficult labor, because of the war and perhaps after just giving birth to her eleventh child, she was very weak. She also lacked the proper nutrition and vitamins." Between tears, father told us, "I was terrified when her legs became paralyzed after Benjamin was born and the doctor said that she had 'beri-beri', not knowing exactly what was wrong with her". Thankfully, my mother recovered well after her labor and survived the ordeal.

"We could not provide Ben with proper nutritional food. Everything was in short supply because of the war and he was not given enough good food as a baby. We had to feed him lots of potatoes, which caused his protruding stomach," recalled my mother. "As a result, Benjamin lost all his teeth and had to live most of his adult life having to use his full upper and lower dentures for his food," she added.

Even as a young child, Benjamin demonstrated his talents as a stage performer. My parents used to say, "Perhaps our Benjamin will be the next preacher in the family, maybe the one after father's own heart." Their remark proved to be true. While going through college, Ben felt God's calling to be a preacher, just like his older brother, John.

With a determination to make his life count, Ben found his way to New Zealand for higher studies and from there he went on to college in Iowa. He did his graduate studies at Garrett Theological Seminary in Evanston, Illinois as he prepared himself for God's work. He became ordained as a Methodist minister and he married his wife Flora Idea. He then served as a pastor in two churches in the Iowa Conference of the United Methodist Church before his appointment by the Bishop as Assistant General Secretary in the Methodist Board of Pension.

Ben and Flora were blessed with three wonderful and godly children, two daughters Anna-Marie, Grace-Kathryn and a son, Peter-Ben. His remarkable life, though sadly cut short by cancer at the young age of 42, has left a legacy to his children to emulate. They have turned out to be successful young professional who also love God and who walk closely with the Lord. Ben's life was a great testimony of God's faithfulness, and his life is a source of inspiration to many whose lives have been touch by him humble spirit, friendliness, he will always be remembered for his loving kindness

His career in the Methodist Board of Pensions was short lived as cancer ravaged his body and ruined his life. Ben was called home to be with the Lord on Christmas Eve in 1986. He left behind his beloved wife Flora, children and his brothers and sisters. He was laid to rest after a solemn and glorious funeral service at the United Methodist Church in Glenview, Illinois. The Methodist Board of Pension has dedicated the Meditation Room in the Board's offices in memory of the Rev. Benjamin Hang.

PERSONAL TESTIMONIES

 A mong the many "life-threatening" and "life-changing"
episodes in the life of my family, as well as my "Even
Dozen" siblings, I have singled out the 5 major and significant
"miraculous events" in the following pages. By no means do
they represent the complete picture, except as a means to serve
as a manifestation of God's omnipresence and divine power in
directing and orchestrating our lives and destiny.

These abbreviated short testimonies truly describe those
"life-threatening" and "life-changing" miraculous events that
took place over the years, and they are truly testimonies of our
faith and trust in a gracious and loving heavenly Father who
loves and sustains us.

They are humbly presented herein mainly to "Glorify God"
and not, in any way, to be anything but to honor and give glory
to God. It is the author's prayerful hope that these personal
testimonies will serve as an inspiration and encouragement to
many, as they journey through life's challenging
circumstances.

CHAPTER 25
MIRACLE #1
MY LIFE SAVED BY ICE!

This is a story of how as a 4-year old boy, I was miraculously saved from the "jaws of death"! It is my greatest testimony and it manifests to God's loving grace and mercy that heals and restores life, and I am alive to tell this story, to give all the glory to the Lord

It was in the early 1930s, and I was about 4 years old. My younger sister had suffered from an intestinal infection and lost the battle for her life for no other reason other than the fact that there was no effective cure for her diarrhea. To me, her death was a tragic and needless loss from lack of proper medication! Not too long after, I found myself fighting for my life as well.

According to my mother, "He had a very high fever and we could not find an effective means or medicine to bring his high temperature down to a safe level. He was becoming delirious due to the high fever. Our church parishioners prayed fervently for this little boy, our son. We were very worried and did not know how else to deal with his serious illness. But our missionary friends, Rev. and Mrs. Gerald Summers cared enough to come to our rescue, to pray for him and to help us"

Even though they were not medical doctors, when the summers saw the serious situation we were in, they immediately knew what to do. They told my parents, "Go quickly and find some ice – ice cubes or ice blocks, whatever, as long as it is ice! Go and get it quickly before it is too late! Meanwhile keep him as comfortable and cool as possible by fanning him and wiping his face with a wet towel" As soon as my father found the ice and brought it home, the Summers went to work on me.

At that time, most Asians in that part of the world had no access to modern medication, partly due to the very high cost of the so-called "western" medicine and partly due to their apparent ignorance. It was a common practice to seek advice from the Chinese medicine man that would prescribe some form of herbal mixture. In many cases, the medicine man never even saw or examined the patient! His knowledge of the different herbs as well as his experience was believed to be adequate to treat any illness.

When a person was seriously ill and could not be cured, or could die, those who were superstitious or non-Christians believed that the sickness was an act of the evil one. As believers in Jesus Christ, the Son of the Living God, my parents believed in the power of fervent prayer and in the miraculous healing power of Jesus Christ. They also sought medical help from their missionary friends and medical practitioners even though modern medicine was non-existent at that time.

When ice was found and brought to the house, the Summers immediately went to work on me while my parents watched in awe and continued praying for my recovery. "You just have to keep him cool by sponging him continuously with an ice cold towel, or you could even bathe him in ice cold water" the Summers told my parents. Thus, by doing that, I was literally saved from the "jaws of death" by the simple use of ice and lots of prayer! God indeed sent His "angels" when the Summers came to save my life!

However, my parents were skeptical then and they could not believe what they had just witnessed. The practice of using ice or ice-cold treatment for a child with very high fever was unthinkable in those days, according to the Oriental way of thinking. At that time, the only way my parents knew how to deal with a sick child was to pray to God for His mercy and healing or by the use of the time-tested Chinese herbal medicines. Even the qualified doctors in those days in Asia were apparently ignorant of modern-day medicine and methods of medical practice.

I believe that it was God's mercy and grace that brought the Summers to our home to pray for me and recommended the ice treatment to my parents. "You were critically ill and near hysteria," my parents recalled, but then they also thought that their American friends were out of their mind to resort to the use of ice! They thought that by subjecting a child to an icy cold bath, it not only would be traumatic but could also cause death to the child. But they were proved to be wrong. Praise the Lord!

Thus I consider this miraculous event to be the greatest testimony of my life. It is truly a testimony of God's loving touch upon my life, as He has allowed me to "walk through the valley of the shadow of death" and to live a life worthy of His great love and grace, and to honor and glorify the Name of Jesus.

It is my heart's desire to share this testimony with everyone, so that it will be a blessing to many, both believers as well as non-believers, in the hope that it will strengthen their faith and uplift them as they struggle to live a life worthy of His mercy and loving grace. Indeed, God works in mysterious ways to bless and sustain everyone who walks in faith and believes in His Word.

CHAPTER 26
MIRACLE #2
THE "FISH TAIL" ACCIDENT

This is a story of a miraculous event that could have taken my life and that of my two daughters. I was driving an over-loaded trailer through the hilly and winding roads of Missouri when it happened. It reminds us that our loving Heavenly Father is always watching and protecting His children.

My two daughters and I were working in Chicago at that time, while my wife, Doris, and two other children remained in Tulsa, Oklahoma. We had vacated our house and Doris had moved into an apartment. With the help of our friends, we had loaded a U-haul trailer full of things to bring to Chicago.

By the time we were ready to leave Tulsa, it was late in the evening as we geared ourselves for the long 12-hour drive to Chicago. Aware that it would not be safe to drive too fast towing a trailer, we were prepared for the longer-than-usual drive. Not having done this before, we were unaware of the dangers of towing an overloaded trailer, especially on the hilly and winding roads through the Ozarks in Missouri.

My eldest daughter, Debbie, a steady and "faster-than-dad"

driver drove the first part of the trip, where the highway was relatively level and straight. When we got to northern Missouri, she started feeling tired and decided that I should take over the wheel. I took over the driving around midnight, driving at my usual safe and slow speed of about 60 mph.

Within a few minutes, it felt as if some strong wind or unusual force was causing the trailer to sway left and right, like a pendulum swinging on a horizontal plane! I thought to myself, "The weather is clear and there isn't any rain, fog and anything on the highway that could cause the vehicle to sway like this. I'm not even driving at a fast speed. There is no reason for the vehicle to act like that."

Before I could realize what was happening, the vehicle started fish-tailing out of control! I let go of the gas pedal quickly, praying that nothing serious would happen. I had lost control of the car and held on tightly to the steering wheel, not knowing what else to do. Debbie, who was sleeping in the back seat woke up at that point. Wrapping her arms around my neck, she exclaimed,

"Oh my goodness, what is happening? Daddy, what is going on? Oh God, please save us!" Meanwhile, my other daughter, Phoebe, who was sitting beside me in the passenger seat simply prayed, "God, have mercy on us. Please help us and take control of the situation! Whatever is happening and wherever we are, we know that you are in control of everything!"

My heart was beating so fast that it was literally "throbbing in my throat". In total shock, all I could do was wait for the vehicle to slow down or come to a stop. Not too long after, we came to a stop, after the car had made a complete 180 degrees turnaround, on the shoulder of the highway. We were told later that the weight of the trailer had made the vehicle spin, thus pulling the car backwards, so that I could not see where we were heading!

When the car stopped, my daughters and I sat there speechless and totally shaken up. It then dawned on us that we were in the middle of nowhere, helpless and hungry! We said a quick prayer to the Lord, thanking Him for protecting us from getting killed. We then prayed for guidance as to what to do next.

When I finally looked out the car window, I noticed that we were resting on the shoulder of the highway, barely 20 feet away from the edge of the shoulder. I could not see anything beyond that. As I got out of the car, to my total shock, I saw that it was a steep edge as the ground sloped downhill. Realizing that we could easily have driven off the edge and gotten killed, I told the girls, "We need to thank God that we did not go beyond the edge of the shoulder, or else we could have rolled off the cliff!"

Who knows what could have happened if we had driven over the cliff and down the slope with the loaded trailer! One can only conclude that it was the work of the Holy Spirit in orchestrating the whole episode. He had been in total control of the bad situation! In desperation, we had prayed out to God, "Please help us! Please show us what to do and please send your angels to our rescue!" and God had answered our prayers! The Holy Spirit was there when we called upon God for His mercy and help.

To our relief, a total stranger stopped to help us. He exclaimed, "What happened? Why are you driving in the wrong direction? Actually, why are you sitting on the shoulder and facing the wrong direction of the highway!" He then told us not to do anything until he returned.

When he returned, he told us, "I had to drive down the freeway in the opposite direction to send out a warning signal. You see, there were other vehicles, especially 18-wheeler trucks, speeding down the freeway!" With his help, we drove slowly over the median, making a 180-degree turn to bring the car around. After making sure that we were all right, our Samaritan "angel" sent us off on our way. In retrospect, we saw that God had indeed heard our prayers and had sent an angel to our rescue!

CHAPTER 27
MIRACLE #3
THE JAPANESE QUARANTINE

This is about how my father narrowly escaped from death in the hands of the Japanese enemy that occupied Singapore soon after its surrender. He believed that God had miraculously saved him from torture by the enemy and perhaps even death.

Soon after the Japanese Imperial forces conquered and captured Singapore, one of the first acts of atrocity by the enemy was to quarantine all the young and able men. They did this not only to exterminate those men who were English-educated and who had served the cause of the British, but also as in revenge towards the Chinese for the old Sino-Japanese war. It was truly by God's grace and mercy that father escaped the Japanese quarantine and thus was literally spared from the "jaws of death". It was learned many years after the war that the remains of thousands of young men were discovered in mass graves in the remote parts of the island, men that had been mercilessly and brutally murdered!

My father was in his 30s and a prime target for the enemy. According to him, "Every young man was ordered by the

Japanese to go through the long quarantine line in the hot sun and to go through the check point. Everyone was searched and questioned. When my turn came to face the Japanese quarantine officer, I could not converse with him for I could neither speak Japanese or English. I was terrified and had no idea what the Japanese officer would do to me. All I could do was smile, and put on the appearance of an innocent young preacher. I hoped that he would recognize the Bible I was carrying in my hand and realize I was really a 'holy man'.

By carrying the bible and acting 'dumb' and speechless, I was literally saved from the 'jaws of death'. I believe that it was the Holy Spirit that gave me the idea of acting like a clergy and visibly displaying the Holy Bible". By the power of God's divine intervention, the Japanese officer was led to believe that my father must have been some kind of a holy man, someone whom he should be nice to and not harm.

"I saw many young men thoroughly searched and interrogated before they were taken away to another spot in the quarantine camp. They were to wait for transportation that would take them to an unknown destination, perhaps to be imprisoned or sent to their death. I trembled the whole time, not knowing what my fate was and seeing all those young men being taken away, not to be seen again," my father said.

When he returned to the safety of his home, my father was joyous as he related his ordeal to the family. He told us, "I did not know what the Japanese soldiers would do to me. I simply obeyed orders, preparing for the worst. I knew that all I could do was pray for God's mercy and to surrender everything to His will in the face of the enemy. Thank God that my prayers were answered. I must have done the right thing to visibly carry the Bible. It was God's divine power that saved me, thus allowing me to testify to His mercy and love. May all glory and honor be given to the Lord." My father's testimony became the subject of many of his sermons.

CHAPTER 28
MIRACLE #4
"ROLL OUT THE BARREL!"

My daughters, Debbie, age 4, Phoebe, age 3 and I could have been killed by a very unusual car accident while on a weekend visit to Singapore in 1970. God protected us and we survived the accident so that we can testify to His love and mercy.

I was working in Malaysia at that time, and visiting Singapore for the weekend. My mother was at the hospital, and my two daughters and I were on our way there to visit her, one seated beside me in the front, and the other in the back. As I approached the junction of Tiong Bahru Road and Hospital Avenue, a fully loaded truck suddenly came into my view. There wasn't a traffic light there.

As I started to turn onto Hospital Avenue, I saw the truck heading directly for me, with no sign of stopping. At that moment, I thought to myself, "That truck driver does not look like it is going to slow down." Within a split second, several rolls of newsprint paper began rolling off the truck, crashing down the road. One of the rolls headed directly towards my car! By that time, the truck had stopped as the driver realized what was happening. I then heard a loud crashing sound alongside my car.

I sat in the driver's seat, dazed and in shock. I knew something terrible had happened and I was unable to do anything but to pray to God for help. With the help of onlookers, I was pulled out of my car and waited by the roadside for the arrival of an ambulance. By God's grace, none of us were badly injured; the girls suffered a few minor cuts from broken glass that had splattered all over the front seat. I suffered 3 broken ribs and my car was destroyed. I was miraculously spared from death injury.

It was truly a miracle that we survived the accident! It could have taken my life or seriously injured us had it not been for God's loving protection. I was badly shaken and in total shock as I realized that the rolls of heavy paper could have easily fallen directly on my car and crushed me to death! I was taken to the hospital with 3 broken ribs but I thank God that I recovered very quickly with just 2 days' in the hospital for observation and recuperation.

On the next day, the local newspaper clearly showed the car license plate of my Malaysian-registered car, which was totally destroyed by the "freak accident". Some gamblers were even known to be betting on the number of my car license plate, which was "BL 9452" and punters were betting on the 4-digit number "9452"

Looking back, I realized that the rolls of newsprint paper had fallen off the truck when the truck driver swerved his truck as he was turning, causing the rolls of paper to roll off the truck and hit the roadway. The rolls of paper were either not securely tied down, or the driver was driving too fast. Imagine what would happened if the rolls of paper had dropped directly on top of my car! God's angels must have been ever present with us then!

CHAPTER 29
MIRACLE #5
"ESCAPE TO ENDAU"

This is the story of our life-threatening episode that could have taken the lives of my family and I had it not been for God's love and protection over us.

During the Japanese occupation of Singapore when food supply was getting scarce, the Japanese administration evacuated our family to the remote jungles in Endau in Johore, Malaysia. In Endau, we lived in a wooden longhouse. We were ordered to clear the jungles and grow our own food, such as potatoes and vegetables. We became "instant" farmers for a whole year, something entirely new to us.

We traveled to Endau in an open-ended truck, part of a caravan of 9 trucks, commandeered by two Japanese soldiers. As we traveled on narrow roads that cut through the jungles of Johore, at the same time, the Malaysian "underground Communists" were hiding everywhere in the jungle, hidden by the dense undergrowth. Although the bandits were not visible to the Japanese soldiers who were accompanying us, we were in full view of the bandit hiding in the jungles. As our caravan moved along the bandit-infested area, we were ordered to keep our heads down and sit down quietly for our own protection. We were too young to really understand the dangers we were in.

Although everyone was frightened, we remained calm. In order to avoid being shot at by the hiding bandits, our caravan had to move along fast. In fact, we were told that even if they started shooting at us, the driver would not stop moving so as not to be captured by the bandits. As we traveled the first long stretch of the country road, everything seemed normal. My father prayed, "Lord, please protect us and keep us safe as we travel through the dangerous country roads. Please send your angels to be with us and protect us from the enemy, even in the face of imminent danger." Although we tried to relax, we were literally trembling, worrying for our safety.

Before long, one of the soldiers told us that we were entering enemy territory. We were told to lay low and keep our heads down and not to move or make any noise that would attract the bandits' attention. "We have to move fast to get through the dangerous territory and will let you know when the danger is over," said the Japanese soldier. All was quiet except for the shrieks of birds and crickets. A sudden burst of gunfire was heard coming from the direction of the trees and brushes, but the enemy was not to be seen! This was followed by gunshots from both sides of our truck caravan. We huddled together and tried to stay calm, hoping and praying that we would not be hit by the gunshots. The young children were asking, "Are we there yet? Is the danger over?"

When we finally arrived at our destination in Endau, we were told that there was another caravan of 8 trucks behind us. All of the passengers' belongings and food were seized by the bandits and the trucks were set on fire. Only one truck in which we were traveling had escaped! Fortunately, only the Japanese soldiers were killed in the skirmish but the civilians were spared! Thank God that we had miraculously escaped death!

CHAPTER 30
MY IMPRESSIONS OF
THE EVANGELIST DR. JOHN SUNG

I was a 7-year old boy among the huge crowds in Singapore that attended the evangelistic meetings and rallies of the evangelist, John Sung. I got to witness the great revivals that took place in the late 1930's. They were just momentous and fantastic!

In the late 1930's, before World War II, Dr. John Sung Song-Che, a saintly man of God who was called to the ministry of evangelism, visited Singapore on several occasions. Even as a young boy, I was deeply impressed by this evangelist and his dynamic preaching and expounding of the Word. I vividly remember those "earth-shaking" days, when thousands of people gathered to listen to this evangelist and countless more were converted or revitalized by his salvation message.

My impression of John Sung was one filled with fear and trembling. He would pound the podium and exclaim in a loud booming voice, "You must repent of your sins! You must believe in Jesus Christ and ask for your sins to be forgiven! You must live a clean and righteous life in order to enter the Kingdom of Heaven! Your only hope of salvation is in Jesus

Christ!" His voice could be heard loud and clear even though no audio system was used.

As I went from one meeting to another with my parents, I marveled at the way the evangelist conducted the meetings. He was able to arouse everyone. The audience was always captivated by Dr. Sung's dynamic message and his powerful prayers for salvation. In the middle of his preaching, he would often ask the congregation to sing songs that were relevant to his message. Many of the songs were written by the evangelist himself. The atmosphere was always charged with great urgency, much like on the day of Pentecost!

One characteristic of Dr. Sung's evangelistic meetings was the "pre-service" audience singing sessions, participated by everyone. These sessions were very lively, as people sang praise songs that were mostly composed by Dr. Sung himself. There was a song leader who would teach everyone a new song on every occasion, rehearsing it repeatedly until everyone had it memorized. Many of those songs became favorites and reminded people of Dr. Sung's evangelistic missions, even to this day!

As Dr Sung preached, he often displayed great sorrow and despair, pounding the podium or falling to the stage floor. He appeared to be in great agony when he led the congregation in fervent prayer, unashamedly crying in the Spirit. At times, his prayers lasted as long as one hour. His prayers were often, "Lord, have mercy on us! Forgive us of our sins! Save us from our wrongful ways! Help us to be more humble – to love you and to serve you! Have mercy on our loved ones – especially the unsaved and lead them to your saving grace and salvation. Save us from falling into eternal hell" As long as his prayers were, his sermons lasted even longer!

Dr. Sung's unique evangelist style left a deep impression on many, even a young boy such as I. There was a sense of urgency in his voice when he gave the altar call to repentance. His desperate cry for repentance resulted in many being convicted of their sins and answering to the alter calls, often in tears. Above the corporate and individual prayers being said, the choir and congregation could be heard singing gospel songs. As a result of Dr. Sung's ministry and evangelist meetings held by him, thousands were converted to Christianity and delivered from the bondage of sin and oppression. Converts, energized by their new-found faith, reached out to relatives, friends and neighbors, and as a result, many others were saved.

Dr. Sung taught that the key to reaching out to the unsaved was to impress upon new converts to form small evangelistic bands and spread the good news of salvation that way. Many formed street evangelism teams, marching through the city with banners displaying messages of salvation and redemption, and singing gospel songs. These teams carried out their mission with great zeal and enthusiasm, pictures of them often shown on local newspapers and other news media. They really made a great impact on the local community and the church.

Dr. Sung's followers were characterized by their strong dedication to living a pure and sanctified life. They displayed strict self-discipline and led a simple lifestyle. They were also committed to living a life of purity and strict obedience to biblical principles. As such, there were strict rules regarding their daily dress code. Men had to wear white shirts and black (or dark) pants, and women had to wear white long "cheong-sums" (a long full-length dress) or a white blouse and pants. Women were not allowed to wear any cosmetic make-up, wear fancy shoes or have fancy hairdos. These were just some of the strict rules of conduct they were required to follow.

Other rules of conduct were related to their day-to-day activities. Gambling and using foul language were considered sinful. Even going to the movies was frowned upon and strongly discouraged as it was thought to corrupt one's mind. Regarding Sunday activities, buying food or any non-essential object was strictly forbidden. As a result of the many rules, Dr. Sung's followers became examples for family and friends to emulate.

News of Dr. Sung's evangelistic work and the activities of his followers often made it on the news media in Singapore and South East Asia. Because of the many lives dramatically changed and converted, Dr. Sung left a legacy for many to "keep the torch burning" and to continue his work among thousands of Christians in Asia. Dr. Sung's many followers became known for their great faith, piety and dedication to God in their daily devotion, prayers and bible study. Till this day, many of his followers still bear witness to Dr. Sung's evangelistic work in Asia.

CHAPTER 31
OUR MOTHERLAND CHINA – MY FIRST IMPRESSIONS

For the first time in my life, I had the opportunity to see my motherland, China, in December 2000. It was an experience that opened my eyes and gave me a glimpse into my family roots in China, where my parents emigrated from in 1927.

I never thought that I would ever have the opportunity to know my family roots in China. My parents used to tell us, "Our hometown village in Fukien, China is so rich in history, that you should see everything for yourselves some day." I never imagined that I would be blessed to see that become a reality. In December of 2000, I had that opportunity as I joined a church group traveling to China, dedicating the newly-built church in my parent's home village of Sienyu City, in the Fukien Province of China.

After months of preparation by the leaders of my father's Hinghwa Methodist Church in Singapore, a group of 33, including my sister Ruth and I, gathered at the Singapore International Airport to fly to Xiamen (also known as Amoy), a seaport on the southern coast of China. On the 4-hour flight from Singapore in a Boeing 737 jet, we were impressed by the professional appearance of the crew and were treated royally. Everyone commented, "I can't believe that China is so advanced! They even fly us in a modern jet and their service is comparable to the best in modern aviation!"

We were surprised at the size of the airport at Xiamen City. Because it was the southern gateway to China, as well as the departure point for flights to various parts of China, including Guangdong, Beijing and Shanghai, the airport was both large and modern. At the airport, we were greeted by a church delegation from Sienyu City. They carried a huge red banner reading, "Welcome Christian friends to China, to our big celebration!" What a warm reception it was for us, being first time visitors to China!

Once we were over with the bureaucratic formalities, our host told us that they had chartered two buses to take us on the 5-hour drive on the modern toll road from Xiamen to Sienyu City. But first lunch had been arranged for us at a local restaurant, what a welcome lunch it turned out to be! It was a delicious10-course lunch! Our host then told us, "When you are finished with your lunch, please re-board the bus and we'll take you on a sight-seeing tour of Xiamen City before going onto the toll way."

For many of us who were first-time visitors to China, it was quite an introduction! Driving through the busy streets of Xiamen, we saw many sights we had never seen before. The streets were crowded with pedestrians and hordes of cyclists pushing their way through the busy streets. Very few vehicles were seen on the roads, and because there weren't any traffic lights, their loud horns were sounded continuously so that they could move through the busy streets!

As we drove around, our bus conductor pointed out to the interesting sights. "See those flatted factories which are 3-4 storey buildings, with no elevator, where thousands of workers are busy at work. They produce all kinds of goods, mostly for export to other countries. Those meat sellers with all those freshly slaughtered chicken and pork, they have to be sold since there is no refrigeration. Whatever is not sold by the end of the day, has to be cooked or it would be ruined! Some vegetables can be sold the next day but others would have to be cooked as well."

Our guide also pointed out the fancy Oriental-styled houses with curved roofs and sun-baked tiled roofs. Most of those buildings were hundreds of years old and many generations lived in the same house as they worked on the farm. Only the more enterprising people ventured out to work in nearby towns; they could not be too far away because there was no to get there except by bicycle. The scenes before me reminded me of old pictures I had seen of China.

There was little traffic on the toll roads except for commercial vehicles and some motor-cyclists who were courageous enough to speed their way alongside the fast-moving vehicles! "The toll roads are very nice! They sure make traveling from one town to another much easier and faster," we were told by our guide, "but the toll fees are very expensive such that only some businesses can afford to pay it and certainly not average motorist! You see, these toll roads were built with large foreign investments. How else could those investors make a profit?"

As we entered Sienyu City, we could see much of the same busy streets, crowded with pedestrians and cyclists as in Xiamen, and with very few vehicles. Unlike the time when my parents were there in the early 1920's, the city had grown into a busy seaport with lots of retail businesses. Much to my surprise, we were even taken to a 5-star hotel, something we did not expect in a small town like Sienyu City!

As our bus pulled up to the hotel, we were greeted with a round of loud crackers, as they welcomed us! There to greet us at the hotel entrance was a sea of faces, comprising mostly of relatives and friends that we had never seen before, except perhaps in some old family photographs! Many of us had never seen our relatives in China, so we did not recognize any faces, even those who were supposedly related to us. Introductions soon began, as people said, "Here, Paul, these are your next of kin from your parents' village in China. You may not know or recognize them but they know who you are because they know your parents." It was quite overwhelming, as we continued to meet our many relatives whose names we hardly knew!

Suddenly, we were approached by two gentlemen in the 50's who introduced themselves as my mother's nephews. We did not recognize their names, except from what we had heard from our parents. Overjoyed, they told us, "We have heard so much of you folks over the many years and can you imagine we are finally meeting you in person! What resemblance you have to your father!" Thereafter, others greeted us with the same salutation. We were introduced to a preacher in his eighties by a couple of ladies. We were told that he was Pastor Lin, my father's old friend. He had known my father very well and was still actively pastoring. We also met the son of our father's sister. We met an 80-year old gentleman, Pastor Goh, who was related to our mother. He knew our parents years ago and became a preacher. During the Communist Government regime, he not only preached but had to farm as well. Although retired, he still preached. Both he and his wife were grateful to have a place to live in the Memorial Tower, which we had helped build as well as the Seven Sisters Church.

We were told to check into our hotel rooms and when properly settled, to go to the main dining area, where a dinner party was waiting for us. What a sumptuous 12-course dinner we were treated to! He also told us, "After your lunch, we'll take you for a bus tour of the city with our guide. You will see Sienyu City, including the site of the old church where your parents belonged to before they were married and left for overseas many years ago."

The next day, we were again driven around for another exciting day. When we arrived at a country church about 20 miles away from Sienyu City, we were again greeted by a round of fire crackers, accompanied by flag-waving and beautifully dressed Sunday School children who formed a guard of honor to welcome us. To them, we were honored visitors from overseas. We were then led to the upper level, above the church sanctuary, to a tea reception where we were served many delicious cakes and local fruits.

From there, we adjourned to the church sanctuary for a special program. Formal greetings were addressed, and there was singing and prayers followed by the presentation of gifts. An exchange of gifts was our host's way of honoring us as their guests. Our gift to them was a piano that was badly needed by the church, and gratefully accepted. With the formal program over, we were entertained to special musical treats and drama, much to the delight and enjoyment of everyone.

The day's program ended with a special dinner feast, prepared for us to show their appreciation for our generosity and Christian love. It seemed like we were continually going from one tea ceremony to another, and from one luncheon to another! In the two days since we arrived, we went from one church celebration to another. Altogether, we had visited seven churches, all within 20 miles of Sienyu City!

This went on for five days until the big day for the celebration of the newly built Seven Steps Christian Church. This Church was built on the same location as the one my parents belonged to when my father was a young seminary student and my mother was "interested to get to know the young would-be preacher," as my father put it. The pastor commented, "It is a very beautiful church with a 7-storey tower, a large sanctuary, a balcony and a lower level Social Hall. It can accommodate as many as four thousand, and is now equipped with an upright piano which you folks donated to us."

The dedication of the newly built Sienyu Church began with a grand thanksgiving celebration on the first day, followed by the dedication service on the second day. The first day ended with a huge banquet for all the VIP's visitors and overseas' visitors, followed by a musical drama and concert, and exchange of gifts. My Uncle Khoo Hock Nam was the leader of our Singapore group and he delivered the speeches and gifts while the church choir performed under the baton of a Beijing-trained musical director. The choir members were resplendent, the ladies dressed in beautiful and colorful red robes, and the men in tuxedos!

When the formal celebration in the sanctuary was over, everyone adjourned to the front courtyard of the church for the ribbon-cutting ceremony. It was a beautiful scene, with the church band playing joyful songs and eight ladies in waiting dressed in colorful red "cheong-sums" (Chinese ladies' long dresses). The ladies each carried a small tray with a pair of scissors, holding the red ribbon stretching 20 feet as they formed a long line. When the prayer by the senior pastor ended, eight VIPs approached the ladies to execute the actual ribbon cutting.

The climax of the ribbon-cutting ceremony was the firing of thunderous crackers that followed. The senior pastor then announced, "We'll take you on a tour of the church building, climb up the 7-storey tower to see the 100-year old church bell, and get a panoramic view of the city. On the way down to the 6th floor, we'll let our two Hang VIPs unveil the plague symbolizing their family gift of the church tower and in memory of their parents, the Rev. and Mrs. Paul Sing-Hoh Hang. We'll also tour the 7-storey Memorial Building right behind the church building and view the Memorial Room on the 3rd floor with all the plagues commemorating all of our Singapore Hinghwa Church friends who donated generously towards this building project." We were very impressed by everything, from the memorable Memorial Room, to the apartments for retired and present pastors on the upper levels, and to the Sunday School and Kindergarten rooms on the lower levels.

On the seventh day of our tour, with the formal church dedication ceremonies behind us, we were free to have the day to make side trips to visit our relatives and next of kin in the villages surrounding Sienyu City. While others dispersed from the hotel, we were escorted by my mother's nephew and niece to see my mother's family mansion and farmland in the village of Nam May, about 20 miles away.

With the escort of a uniformed soldier, a relative of my mother's grand niece, we were driven through narrow roads to the village. As we got out of the car, my mother's nephew said, "This is our family farmland stretching up to the hills and as far as the eye can see! And there in the middle of the farmland stands our age-old Ng family mansion. We'll walk on this dirt road for about 200 feet and over a small wooden bridge to get to the reception area in the courtyard in front of the mansion. As you can see, a few of our family-related members have also built their own 3-storey brick homes back-to-back and adjacent to the family mansion."

After a brief introduction to some of the members of my mother's large family, my sister Ruth and I were treated to a sumptuous lunch at the house. We were told, "You must not be shy but make yourself at home and eat all that you can! After all, this is like your own home as your mother was our great aunt, and you are really considered one of us! It is so wonderful to see you folks for the first time in our life."

Our sumptuous lunch consisted of 10 dishes of home-cooked cuisine, from noodles and steamed fish, to fresh clam soup and delicious stir-fried eels that were produced right on the family farm. There were 30 people seated in two large round tables, and after praying, everyone lifted their chopsticks and ate. "Come let's eat and be merry! Let's drink to our guests, our long lost cousins who have come all the way from overseas to see us for the first time!" someone exclaimed. With that toast, everyone dipped their spoons and chopsticks into the common bowls of soup and dishes of food! We felt somewhat uncomfortable seeing everyone digging into the food, but then realized that such was the common practice in China with most families.

Soon after dessert was served, all the men began pushing

and offering cigarettes to everyone as a gesture of courtesy. Smoking cigarettes is a favorite habit for most of the men, from young teenagers to older men. Everywhere we went, we saw men smoking heavily, including streetwalkers, household men and workers at the hotel desks. Even the bus driver and his accompanying conductor smoked on the job! One wonders how the men in China can look so healthy and slim!

The climax of our visit to my mother's mansion was the photo-op gathering of over 60 relatives in the front courtyard. We were surrounded by a sea of faces, all of whom were my mother's next of kin, but total strangers to us, as we were to them, but proud claiming to be related to us. There were adults in the 40-50's, a large number of young boys and girls, and one elder lady of 90 years who was said to be related to mother.

The family farmland had lots of vegetable and rice fields. My mother's nephew told us, "We grow a large variety of vegetables of our own so there is no need to buy any from the market. We also have lots of pigs, chickens and ducks as you can see them grazing all over the land. So you see, we are quite self sufficient when it comes to basic foodstuffs to live on. But we are not wealthy since only few of us are able to work outside the family farmland for extra income and our farm produce sells for little money."

He continued telling us, "A few of our young nephews got the great idea from reading and studying books, of producing eels on our farmland. The idea worked well. As you can see, we are able to reproduce lots of eels in our own aquarium. We feed the eels with our farm produce and they multiply very well. We produce the eels mainly for export to Japan and also for our own consumption. There is a good market for eels in Japan but unfortunately it has not been profitable after the devaluation of the Japanese yen."

We were then taken on a tour of the large family mansion, boasting of as many as 20 rooms that can accommodate a large number of families. "In the old days, all of the Ng clan family lived in the same mansion and worked on the family farm," he said. As we walked through the dark corridors, he pointed out, "This is where the family living room used to be. It is very much neglected now filled with old furniture, earthenware and all kinds of stuff lying everywhere as nobody wants it. Not too many families live here now." We were then shown a small dark room at the back of the family room that, according to him, was my mother's bedroom. "Some of us who work outside the farm are financially able to build our own homes, like those five brick houses you see by the side of the mansion. It costs us less to build our own homes on this land than to build outside the family farmland. It is a simple but healthy life for us."

On the second last day of our visit to Sienyu City, we teamed up with a few fellow travelers from Singapore for a one-day tour of Foochow city, about 150 miles away. We later learned that we had overpaid our two taxi drivers. As we drove along the toll roads to Foochow, our tour guide said, "See those high mountains ahead of us? We'll drive around the mountains and go along the coast to see the beautiful historic city of Foochow, which is right across the sea from Taiwan."

Foochow is a beautiful city with many tourist landmarks, museums, historic gardens, and famous old palaces and temples. Foochow is also a busy industrial city with many manufacturing businesses, making it a thriving industrial seaport. Leaving Foochow, we saw the marvelous suspended bridge that spanned across the Foochow River. In Foochow, we got to taste the delicious Foochow food that was very inexpensive.

On our final day in China, we again traveled by chartered bus from Sienyu City back to Xiamen for a day's visit, before flying back to Singapore. Uncle Khoo, who was our chief tour organizer, told us, "Amoy is a very old and interesting city with a lot of history. You do not want to miss the opportunity to see this ancient but bustling seaport. It has been a gateway to southern China. We will be staying at the Singapore Hotel which is owned by a Singapore investor. As soon as you are settled in the hotel and finished eating your breakfast, we must leave for the harbor to catch the ferry across to the famous island resort. There, you will see many art effects and beautiful architecture that Foochow is well-known for." We did indeed enjoy a memorable day in Foochow.

We reluctantly headed back to the Xiamen Airport to board our flight back to Singapore, thus ending our enjoyable and memorable 9-day visit to China. It was an experience of a lifetime for many of us! Upon our return to Singapore, everyone was excited to share their experiences, with lots of pictures and videos. We found ourselves saying, "China is a wonderful place to visit; we must make another trip there, after all, it is such a huge and marvelous country!"

VISITING OUR MOTHERLAND IN CHINA

Front View of 7-Storey Church & Bell Tower

Dedication of the Newly-Built Hinghwa Church
Sienyu City, P.R.C. – Dec. 25, 2000

Uncle Khoo, Ruth and Paul with relatives inside the sanctuary

The Sienyu Church Choir at the New Church Building Dedication

Sienyu Church Pastors presenting gift to Hinghwa Methodist Church, Singapore.

OUR MOTHERLAND CHINA – MY FIRST IMPRESSIONS

Visit to Mother's "Nam May" Village longhouse with part of the large village "clan"

Ruth & Paul with some of Mother's relatives

Visiting Foochow on a 1-day tour with Mom's nephew "Yung Ming" (left)

Memorial to Father & Mother
in the Memorial Building behind the Sienyu Church

AFTERWORD

It was ten years ago that I decided to write about my life's adventures and unique experiences, both in Singapore and in America. Since then, I have been encouraged by family and friends to publish my autobiography (previously entitled, "We will glorify the Lord!" hence this book entitled, "Blessings by the Dozen!" As I began with my researching and writing of my book of memoirs, I have further researched and have been blessed with an even greater insight and deeper understanding of my life, as well as the "Hang" family roots and my entire 12 siblings' families everywhere.

My wife, Doris, and I have been greatly blessed in our 40 years' of marriage, and our four wonderful children have individually been blessed with good, successful education and careers as they continue to walk in the Lord. We have all been blessed with good health and a great family, as we continue to trust in God's loving grace and faithfulness, and living the so-called "American Dream".

Our three daughters, Debbie Harms, Phoebe Fung and Dr. Muriel Burk are married to their wonderful husbands, John Harms, Alan Fung and Keith Burk. They have been blessed with great families of their own, and are well and living the "American Dream". In their own unique ways, they each look to the Lord for wisdom and guidance as they continue to serve Him. Our son, Dr. Timothy Hang is a dental surgeon and he is faithfully serving the Lord at the Life Changers Church in Hoffman Estates, Illinois. We are very proud of our children, their academic and vocational accomplishments.

We are greatly blessed with eight wonderful grandchildren who bring us great joy and fulfillment, even though, of necessity, they do not live very close to us. I am legally retired and I am truly thankful to the Lord for having been blessed with relatively good health. We cherish the many opportunities to visit our children and their families, though with Doris being employed part time, we do not visit them as often as we would like to. Of course, we are thrilled when they do come and visit us from time to time also.

The history of the "Hang" family is one that is filled with many life-changing episodes and challenging circumstances through which God, in His love and mercy, has caused His will to be accomplished in our lives. Indeed, God has greatly blessed everyone in the lineage of my family. Following the migration of my parents from China to Singapore in 1927, our family tree has expanded "exponentially" from twelve siblings to over 120 souls living across the globe from Singapore to Hong Kong, to Australia, to London and the United States of America.

My eldest sister, Mary, is married to Dr. Robert C. K. Loh. They live in Singapore with their sons, Stephen and Andrew Loh. Patricia, their daughter lives in Hawaii with her husband, Stephen Chew. Her children are all married and they have been blessed with successful careers and a wonderful life in Singapore. Bob and Mary have five grandchildren, bringing them great joy and fulfillment in their "golden" years. Mary and Bob are semi-retired, he from his years of practice in his Eye Center Clinic in Singapore. Having completed her nursing career, she has been helping Bob in his Eye Clinic for many years. Robert Loh continues to be active in various local and community affairs.

Ruth, my second sister, is retired, having worked as a nurse her entire life and volunteers her time at the Ling Kwang Home for Senior Citizens in Singapore. Her daughter, Aileen, is married to Dr. Albert Pang and lives in Dallas, Texas with their two sons, Phillip and David, and daughter, Allison. In her retirement, Ruth is blessed with relatively good health and a strong desire to travel and to reach out to the needy.

Peter, my eldest brother, went home to be with the Lord in 1961, after his prolonged battle with cancer at age 31. He worked as a Southeast Asia Representative for Prentice-Hall International, a well-known American publishing company, after receiving his two degrees from Oregon State University in 1959.

My sister, Rebecca, married Dr. Wong Kong Meng of Malacca and lived till the age of 68, when she left us very suddenly after a short illness in Adelaide, Australia. She and her husband have been blessed with four children, Carolyn Radford, Lye-Kheng Yap, Alan and Andrew Wong. Their daughters, Carolyn and Lye-Kheng, are medical practitioners working in their father's family practice. Their eldest son, Alan Wong, is an attorney and their other son, Andrew, is a chartered accountant. The entire family migrated to Adelaide, Australia in 1981.

Esther McKinley, another sister, is retired after being a schoolteacher for over 30 years in Singapore and in Michigan. She married Dr. Robert McKinley, a professor at Michigan State University in East Lansing, Michigan. Esther's daughter, Susan Jed, is a highly skilled interior designer in Washington, D.C. Susan and her husband, Timothy, are avid travelers and have spent many vacations in Europe as well as here in the United States. They live in Arlington, Virginia and are blessed with good health and challenging careers. Her son, Dr. Steven McKinley, is finishing his residency at Baylor School of Medicine in Houston, Texas, specializing in Ophthalmology. He plans to marry Dr. Pooja Varshney, a pediatrician in the spring of 2006. She is finishing her residency as well.

My younger sister, Sarah, lives in Hong Kong with her husband Dr. Eddie Chan and their three children, Eugene, Edwin and Elaine. Their children are married and they live in close proximity to their parents. Eddie has had his own dental practice for many years and now their son, Eugene, is a dental surgeon at the same practice. Sarah and Eddie are enjoying their semi-retirement, as well as their five grandchildren.

John, my younger brother, and his wife Irene Ong have two sons, Martin and Alvin, and a daughter, Karen. They are blessed with good jobs with the Singapore Government. Martin's wife is Julia and Karen's husband is Samuel. They continue to do well in Singapore despite having lost their beloved father in 1982. They have been blessed with a good life in Singapore and remain faithful in the Lord.

Elizabeth, my younger sister is an accomplished pianist who has taught piano for over 45 years. She is married to Samuel Kwan, an electrical engineer who came from an old and distinguished Singapore family. They, too, decided to immigrate to the United States in 1985 for the sake of their three sons and they now live in Houston, Texas. Their eldest son, Stanley, works as an information technology specialist at Rice University in Houston, while their second son, Edmund, is an investment banker for JP Morgan Chase in London. He is married to Ellen Chung. Kevin, their youngest, is a creative director and photographer living in New York City. His works are collected in museums and private collections internationally. After successfully battling cancer in 2002, Elizabeth is in stable health and maintains a busy schedule with teaching piano students.

My younger brother, David, was married to Susan Ong. Sadly, David went home to be with the Lord prematurely after a long battle with cancer. They have two daughters, Evelyn Tan and Lydia Tang. Susan is retired and Evelyn and Lydia are busy homemakers. Evelyn and her husband, Gary, have a son, Russell, and they live with Susan in Singapore. Lydia and her husband, Melvin Tang, an electrical engineer, have two daughters, Marissa and Hannah. Lydia and Melvin now live in Adelaide, Australia.

Joseph, the fifth boy, and his wife, Lim Keow Cheng, live in Houston, Texas. He has a successful cruise business that takes him to many places around the world, and when he is not traveling, he loves to play golf. They are blessed with three sons, Jeffrey, Julian and Jeremy, who are all young professionals. Jeffrey works in Singapore while Julian and Jeremy live in Austin, Texas, where they are gainfully employed.

Benjamin, my youngest brother, was married to Flora Idea, and they have three children, Anna-Marie, Grace-Kathryn and Peter-Benjamin. Ben was an ordained Methodist clergy who had served in four Methodist Churches in Iowa. Before Benjamin was called home to be with the Lord in 1986, he was the Assistant General Secretary for the Methodist Board of Pension. All three children are married and live in the greater Chicago area. Their eldest, Anna-Marie, is married to Matt Clausen, and they have three sons, Tristan-Quinn, Talon Benjamin and Shane-Callon. Anna-Marie and Matt are both working for Abbott Laboratories in Illinois. Peter-Ben and his wife, Erica, have a son, Malachi-Benjamin, and a daughter, Kayleigh-Idea. They live in Glenview, Illinois and Peter-Ben works for the General Board of Pension in Evanston, Illinois. Grace-Kathryn, their youngest, and her husband Frank Tessien, are blessed with successful careers and they live in Kenosha, Wisconsin. Ben and Flora have been blessed with five lovely grandchildren who dearly miss their beloved grandparents.

In writing the history of my large family, I am overwhelmed by the formidable and challenging task of accurately documenting everything of significance in our increasingly large family. I hope that nothing of significance has been lost as I try to write about the lives of different family members, including the younger generations. It is my prayer and hope that the younger family members will come forth to "keep the torch burning" so to speak, and to perpetuate our Hang legacy for the future generations.

"Hang" Family Tree

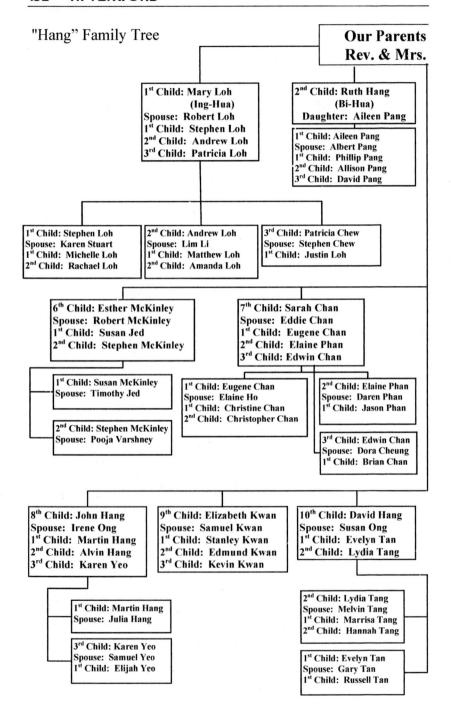

**Our Parents
Rev. & Mrs.**

1st Child: Mary Loh
(Ing-Hua)
Spouse: Robert Loh
1st Child: Stephen Loh
2nd Child: Andrew Loh
3rd Child: Patricia Loh

2nd Child: Ruth Hang
(Bi-Hua)
Daughter: Aileen Pang
1st Child: Aileen Pang
Spouse: Albert Pang
1st Child: Phillip Pang
2nd Child: Allison Pang
3rd Child: David Pang

1st Child: Stephen Loh
Spouse: Karen Stuart
1st Child: Michelle Loh
2nd Child: Rachael Loh

2nd Child: Andrew Loh
Spouse: Lim Li
1st Child: Matthew Loh
2nd Child: Amanda Loh

3rd Child: Patricia Chew
Spouse: Stephen Chew
1st Child: Justin Loh

6th Child: Esther McKinley
Spouse: Robert McKinley
1st Child: Susan Jed
2nd Child: Stephen McKinley

7th Child: Sarah Chan
Spouse: Eddie Chan
1st Child: Eugene Chan
2nd Child: Elaine Phan
3rd Child: Edwin Chan

1st Child: Susan McKinley
Spouse: Timothy Jed

2nd Child: Stephen McKinley
Spouse: Pooja Varshney

1st Child: Eugene Chan
Spouse: Elaine Ho
1st Child: Christine Chan
2nd Child: Christopher Chan

2nd Child: Elaine Phan
Spouse: Daren Phan
1st Child: Jason Phan

3rd Child: Edwin Chan
Spouse: Dora Cheung
1st Child: Brian Chan

8th Child: John Hang
Spouse: Irene Ong
1st Child: Martin Hang
2nd Child: Alvin Hang
3rd Child: Karen Yeo

9th Child: Elizabeth Kwan
Spouse: Samuel Kwan
1st Child: Stanley Kwan
2nd Child: Edmund Kwan
3rd Child: Kevin Kwan

10th Child: David Hang
Spouse: Susan Ong
1st Child: Evelyn Tan
2nd Child: Lydia Tan

1st Child: Martin Hang
Spouse: Julia Hang

3rd Child: Karen Yeo
Spouse: Samuel Yeo
1st Child: Elijah Yeo

2nd Child: Lydia Tang
Spouse: Melvin Tang
1st Child: Marrisa Tang
2nd Child: Hannah Tang

1st Child: Evelyn Tan
Spouse: Gary Tan
1st Child: Russell Tan

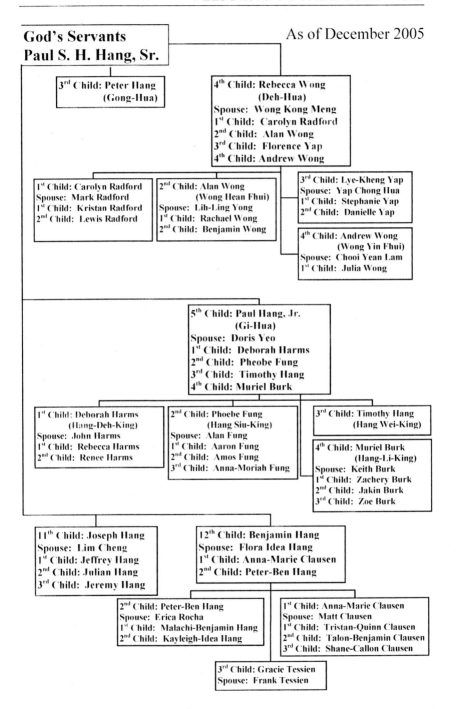

God's Servants
Paul S. H. Hang, Sr.

As of December 2005

3rd Child: Peter Hang
(Gong-Hua)

4th Child: Rebecca Wong
(Deh-Hua)
Spouse: Wong Kong Meng
1st Child: Carolyn Radford
2nd Child: Alan Wong
3rd Child: Florence Yap
4th Child: Andrew Wong

1st Child: Carolyn Radford
Spouse: Mark Radford
1st Child: Kristan Radford
2nd Child: Lewis Radford

2nd Child: Alan Wong
(Wong Hean Fhui)
Spouse: Lih-Ling Yong
1st Child: Rachael Wong
2nd Child: Benjamin Wong

3rd Child: Lye-Kheng Yap
Spouse: Yap Chong Hua
1st Child: Stephanie Yap
2nd Child: Danielle Yap

4th Child: Andrew Wong
(Wong Yin Fhui)
Spouse: Chooi Yean Lam
1st Child: Julia Wong

5th Child: Paul Hang, Jr.
(Gi-Hua)
Spouse: Doris Yeo
1st Child: Deborah Harms
2nd Child: Pheobe Fung
3rd Child: Timothy Hang
4th Child: Muriel Burk

1st Child: Deborah Harms
(Hang-Deh-King)
Spouse: John Harms
1st Child: Rebecca Harms
2nd Child: Renee Harms

2nd Child: Phoebe Fung
(Hang Siu-King)
Spouse: Alan Fung
1st Child: Aaron Fung
2nd Child: Amos Fung
3rd Child: Anna-Moriah Fung

3rd Child: Timothy Hang
(Hang Wei-King)

4th Child: Muriel Burk
(Hang-Li-King)
Spouse: Keith Burk
1st Child: Zachery Burk
2nd Child: Jakin Burk
3rd Child: Zoe Burk

11th Child: Joseph Hang
Spouse: Lim Cheng
1st Child: Jeffrey Hang
2nd Child: Julian Hang
3rd Child: Jeremy Hang

12th Child: Benjamin Hang
Spouse: Flora Idea Hang
1st Child: Anna-Marie Clausen
2nd Child: Peter-Ben Hang

2nd Child: Peter-Ben Hang
Spouse: Erica Rocha
1st Child: Malachi-Benjamin Hang
2nd Child: Kayleigh-Idea Hang

1st Child: Anna-Marie Clausen
Spouse: Matt Clausen
1st Child: Tristan-Quinn Clausen
2nd Child: Talon-Benjamin Clausen
3rd Child: Shane-Callon Clausen

3rd Child: Gracie Tessien
Spouse: Frank Tessien

ACKNOWLEDGEMENT

With my deep appreciation to:
1. My father the late Rev. Paul S. H. Hang Sr. for his book, "My Christian Testimony (1970 edition) that has inspired me to embark on this new "Blessings by the Dozen" book project.
2. My sister, Esther (Hang) McKinley for her loving moral support.
3. My family members for helping me to edit my manuscript and their hard work in checking and proof reading my literary work.
4. My wife and my children for their patience and their understanding of my total commitment to this book project.
5. My Christian friends for their prayerful support for my book project without whose interest and support this book project may not have been possible and blessed beyond my expectation for the glory of God!

ADDENDUM

The pages of this Addendum are Extracts from the book, "My Christian Testimony" written by my beloved father the late Rev. Paul Sing-Hoh Hang Sr. who compiled his book of "Sermons and Essays and Historical Events relating to the Methodist Church in Singapore & Malaysia and the Christian Church in China.

This book was printed in 1969 and donated to the "Churches around the World" by the late Rev. Paul S. H. Hang Sr. with the financial support of his family and friends. These pages were the only pages printed in English. They were painstakingly translated by John Hang and myself in 1970 on behalf of my father.

However, it is the writer's intention to have his father's writings translated into the English language eventually, hopefully to have an English version made and published for general circulation.

Paul Kee-Hua Hang, Jr.

(Extracts from the book, "My Christian Testimony" by the late Rev. Paul Sin-Hoh Hang – Written and printed in Singapore in 1969)

"TO THE GLORY OF GOD AND
FOR THE CONVERSION OF MAN"

THIS BOOK SERVES TO COMMEMORATE:

1. The Eight-Fifth (85th) Anniversary (1885 – 1970) of the Methodist Church in Singapore and Malaysia;
2. The Sixtieth (60th) Anniversary (1911 – 1970) of the Hinghwa Methodist Church, Singapore;
3. The Thirty-Fifth (35th) Anniversary (1936 – 1970) of the Chinese Annual Conference in Singapore / Malaysia.
4. The one Hundredth (100th) Anniversary (1870 – 1970) of the Birth of my Parents, Mr. Hang Hu-Bu and Mrs. Hang Hu-Bu (Deng Do-Di)

"…And as a Gift to God's Church throughout the World."

Rev. & Mrs. Paul Sing-Hoh Hang

Paul Sing-Hoh Hang and Rachel Ng So-Ging - 2–1–1971

TABLE OF CONTENTS

Matthew 1:21, Luke 2: 18-14
12. The wounded Christ heals Mankind
    Isaiah 53: 5
13. Christ in the Garden of Gethsamane
    Matthew 26: 36-46
14. "A Corn of Wheat Dies and Bringeth forth Much Fruit
    John 12: 24
15. God comes First in our Lives
    I Colossians 1: 18
16. We would See Jesus!
    John 12: 21
17. We want Jesus Christ
    John1:38
18. We Must Uphold Jesus Christ
    John 3:14, 15
19. We should hold on to Jesus Christ
    Solomon 3: 4
20. I treasure the Knowledge of Jesus Christ
    Philippians 3: 7-8
21. The Blood of Jesus Christ Saves Us
    Hebrews 9: 22
22. Seek Ye the Peace of God
    John 14: 27
23. God fulfills your Faithful Prayer
    Matthew 8: 3, 17, 13
24. The timely seizure of your Golden Opportunity
    Ephesians 5: 16
25. The Good Example of Abraham's Servant
    Genesis 24: 26, 27
26. Prayer – the Prelude to the Ministry of the Word
    Acts: 6:4
27. Our Duty to Proclaim Christ's Gospel
    I Corinthians9:17 .28
28. Our Need to Work Abundantly for the Lord
    I Corinthians 15: 58
29. The Secret of Happiness-No Misery, No Anxiety

II Kings 7: 9
30. Labour Earnestly for your reward in the Kingdom of Heaven
    Matthew 11: 12
31. "Honour thy father and thy mother"
    Exodus 20: 12
32. Eternal Life surpasses all Worldly Gains
    Matthew 16: 26
33. What shall we do to inherit Eternal Life?
    Matthew 19:16
34. The Faithful shall be Healed
    Matthew 9: 21
35. Pray on your knees to do God's Work
    Isaiah 54: 2

V. HISTORICAL ESSAYS
   1. The Place of Christianity in China.
   2. A Biography of John Wesley.
   3. A Century of Methodism in China.
   4. 85 Years' of Methodism in Singapore and Malaysia.
   5. The 60-Year History of the Hinghwa Methodist Church in Singapore.
   6. A Brief History of the Singapore Chinese Inter-Church Union.
   7. A Short History of the Evangelist Dr. John Sung.
   8. 35 Years of the Singapore Christian Evangelistic League.
   9. Malaysia Chinese Annual Conference -35 Years in Perspective
   10. Founding of the Unique Hakka Methodist Church – A Brief History.

VI. ESSAYS ON CHRISTIAN THEOLOGY AND CHRISTIAN LIVING
    1. What shall we dedicate to celebrate Christmas?
    2. The Christian's contribution towards Christmas.

3. Jesus is the Wonderful Christ.
4. The Disciple John's concept of Jesus Christ.
5. My conception of Jesus Christ.
6. The cross of Jesus Christ.
7. The Crucifixion.
8. Christ's Resurrection.
9. My Conviction of Christ's Passion and Resurrection.
10. The Revelation – that is, the Second Coming of Christ.
11. Glorify God whilst preaching the message of Salvation to others.
12. We need Spiritual Power.
13. My Christian Belief in the Scriptures.
14. A Study of Prayer.
15. A Study of Christian Education.
16. Christ and His Children.
17. A Discussion on Children and Parents.
18. The Christian Family's Responsibility towards Children.
19. My idea of Christian Youth.
20. The relevance of the Christian Church in Youth.
21. Mutual relationship in the Christian Family.
22. A Study of the Christ-Cultured Family.
23. A Study of Family Ethics.
24. The Christian's Perspective of War.
25. Christianity and the Atom Bomb.
26. Christianity versus Society.
  a. New Life for the Christian.
27. What is Expected of the Christian's Knowledge.
28. The Christian should preserve the Precious Virtues.
29. The Conditions of being A Christian.
30. The ways of a Good Christian.
31. The Revived Church in A Renewed Personality.
32. My views on the matter of Heaven and Hell.
33. A account of my preaching experience.
34. I desire the whole family to worship our Heavenly Father.

VII. ESSAYS ON MY TRAVELS

1. My Tour Around the World in 1948
2. My Impressions of the General Conference at Boston, U.S.A.1948
3. A Brief Report of My Return Visit to China in 1936.

VIII.EVENTS OF JOY
1. "The 40th Wedding Anniversary Celebration of Rev. & Mrs. Paul S. H. Hang"

By: Rev. Fang Chao Hsi
2. "Advanced Age in the Eyes of God"

By: Rev. James T. S. Ling

IX. EPILOGUE
1. Extending the Kingdom of God.
2. To the Glory of God for the Conversion of Man.
3. "I will declare What He hath done for my Soul"
4.My Reflections on the book "My Christian Testimony"

By: Rev. Quek Keng Hoon
5. My Reflections on those messages of Rev. Paul Sing-Hoh Hang

By: Mr. Gideon Chen.

范新福牧師仇儷與新嘉坡友誼企業有限公司部份職員合影
一九七一年一月十一日

A Group Picture of the Publishing Team w/Rev. & Mrs. Paul S. H. Hang Sr.

"NEW YEAR, NEW HAPPINESS, AND NEW CREATURE"
BY: REV. PAUL S. H. HANG, SR.

Scripture Lesson: II Corinthians 5: 1-17

Scripture Text: II Corinthians 5: 17

I take this opportunity to wish you "A Happy New Year" May you be blessed with prosperity in the year 1971.

In the New Year we make many resolutions. For the student, he resolves to achieve Grade I in his examinations. The laborer resolves to work hard and earn more money. The businessman hopes that his business will prosper with bigger turnovers. For the Christian, he resolves to become "A New Creature".

"How can we become a new creature?" we may ask. At this juncture, I am reminded of Paul's words, "Wretched man that I am! Who will deliver me from this body of death?" Only those who are "in Christ" can become a new creature or a new man, those who receive God's plan of salvation. Paul constantly reminded the Christians as well as the non-Christians in his day about this important point. In knowing Christ, our sins are forgiven and we can have fellowship with God, our Heavenly father. Because Christ is righteous, we too can become righteous. "All things are passed away behold old things are become new". Satan has no hold on our lives and the Holy Spirit becomes active in our lives, leading us to attain Christlikeness. Paul says, "I beg you to lead a life worthy of the calling to which you have been called." We are called to become the "sons of God".

I wish to bring up four important aspects of the New Creature:

Firstly, the new man lives in a new house. Paul says, "For we know that if the earthly tent we live in is destroyed, we have a building from God, a house not made with hands, eternal in the heavens. "The earthly tent symbolizes our earthly bodies and the new building symbolizes heaven, the Christian's eternal home. Paul says to the Colossians: "For you have died, and your life is his with Christ in God." Since the day when we received salvation, our souls take its abode in heaven. Our bodies are temporal and it is the heavenly things that we should concern ourselves with. I appeal to you never to neglect to meditate on heavenly things.

John says, "When I (Jesus) go and prepare a place for you, I will come again and will take you to myself, that where I am you may be also."

Secondly, the new man has new aims, that is, to please God in his words, thoughts and deeds. This will result from our past experience and the longer we know Christ, the more we will love Him.

After having known Christ, a chained smoker will eventually give up smoking. With the money saved, he contributes toward the Church expenses. At the same time, he shares with others what Christ has done for him.

Dear readers, from the day we accepted Christ, we should not fail to please God. Paul says, "To present our bodies to be a living sacrifice, holy and acceptable to God, which is our spiritual worship."

Thirdly, a new man leads a new way of life. Paul says, "He dies for all, that those who live might live no longer for themselves but for Him who for their sakes died and was raised"

The new life proceeds from our thinking. Paul says, "For the love of Christ controls us, because we are convinced that one has died for all; therefore, all have died." Christ died that we might live and our old self is buried with Him in the atonement. The old self is nailed to the Cross, the bad self becomes good and pleasing unto God. The new man's centre of life is Christ, the righteous. By so doing, he receives abundant blessings from God.

Fourthly, a new man has new ideas. He becomes aware of the work that he does and whether it will be contrary to his Christian faith. If proved contrary, he will go for another job. We must have the conviction that no matter who we are or what we do, we are ever serving God. Before he became a Christian, a storekeeper was dishonest in his dealings with his regular customers. He would give one or two tahils less, and would charge his customers slightly higher than the shop next door. At the end of the year, he found a balance of great profit at the expense of his customers. After he became a Christian, he decided to have new ideals, one of which was not to cheat the customers. At the end of the financial year, he discovered that he made better profits than ever before.

I studied in the Fukien University in the spring of 1924. At that time, I was in the second year of my studies. On the Chinese New Year's day of that year, I decided to go away alone by myself and to spend some time in meditating on my early childhood days since my birth. I went to a hill nearby and knelt on a stone and began to pray and have fellowship with Christ for about one hour. Having sung a few hymns and read the scripture, memories came back to me of the year 1901, the year when I was born in Sienyu City in Fukien Province. In this city many folks were engaged in farming and timber logging. Eight months after my birth, my father left for Perak, Malaysia to work. I stayed with my mother, Madam Deng Do-Di. She attended the Bible School for woman, and after four years she graduated. During this time, both my parents were 30 years old. Later, my mother became a Bible woman in the

Methodist Church for 21 years. During this time, I helped my mother in the household chores. On Sundays, I worked in the church, tidying up the pews and also helping in the Choir.

From the age of 9 to 22 years, I attended the Guthrie Memorial High School in Putein City, Fukien. I also attended some courses in the Seminary. Still on the hill, I prayed and thanked God for my family upbringing and asked for His guidance on my future work. I prayed thus," Dear God, I thank thee abundantly for thy blessings, I pledge to become a new man. If it is thy will that I should become a minister, I pray thee to reveal thy will through the words of Scripture. In Christ's name I pray, Amen."

Upon opening my eyes, I turned the pages of Scripture and found Romans chapter 9.This chapter relates to the conversion of Saul to Paul. I was filled with joy and I cried out, "Alleluia, praise the Lord!" On descending from the hill, I decided to change my name from Hang Hoh-Gi to Hang Sing-Hoh, and I called myself Paul Sing-Hoh Hang as from then. In the autumn of 1924, I studied the BA. Course at the Nanking Theological Seminary and graduated in 1927 with a B.A. diploma (B.A. course at Nanking Theological Seminary is equivalent to the Fukien University Theology course.)

In April of this year, my wife and I celebrated our 70th birthday. I thank God for His abundant blessings as I recall my past life and experiences. I am reminded of Psalm 103: 3-5, "Who forgives all our iniquity, who heals all my diseases who redeems my life from the pit, who crowns me with steadfast love and mercy, who satisfies me with good as I live so that my youth is renewed like the eagle's."

Through the encouragement I received from my fellow colleagues and friends, I decided to embark on this publication, in thanksgiving unto God and unto Him be glory and praise. The title of this book is, "My Christian Testimony."

I am indebted to the 19 ministers who have so kindly consented to write the different prefaces. I wish to express my sincere thanks to them.

The Methodist Church in Malaysia and Singapore has a history of eighty-five years. I have the privilege to serve this church for 44 years. I am neither a scholar nor a renowned writer. I write this out of my personal experience and hoping that the readers will be encouraged to serve God more dearly and to love Him more dearly also. For the others, I hope that they will be helped by the Holy Spirit to acknowledge God as their personal Savior. This is also to encourage each reader to lead a life worthy of His Holy Name. I pray that we shall receive God's abundant grace in this life and in the world to come life eternal.

Dear brothers and sisters in Christ, may we resolve in this coming year to lead lives which are righteous and to perform works pleasing to God. May we spend more time to meditate on the things of God and seek His abundant blessings. Once again, I wish you a Happy New Year and may it bring new happiness and may we also become new creatures in the sight of God. Amen.

Sermon delivered by: Rev. Paul S. H. Hang.
Interpreted by: John D. H. Hang
February 1970.

MY CHRISTIAN TESTIMONY
PREFACE: BY MRS. GEORGE W. HOLLISTER

"It is a privilege to have a small part in Rev. Paul Hang's 70th Birthday Book of Sermons. His life and that of my husband's have been entwined for 55 of those 70 years. George W. Hollister, born in India of missionary parents, and Mary Brewster, daughter of William N. and Elizabeth Brewster, pioneer missionaries in China, graduated from Ohio Wesleyan University in 1913.After graduation from Garrett Theological Seminary, they were married in Hinghwa, in Fukien, China, in 1915.

We were appointed to Sienyu, Fukien, China where Hang Sing-Hoh was a student in the Methodist Boys' School. His mother was a Bible-woman and traveled the Sienyu District with Miss Martha J.S. Lebeus. She loved to tell about the small boy waiting beside his mother's sedan chair, with his Bible and Hymn book in his hand. "I'm going to deng-do i.e. preach the Gospel." He would say. That small boy did not get to go then, but for a large part of the 70 years since then, Deng-Do, preaching has been his chief love and delight, as it always was for George Hollister, his friend and spiritual father, up to the last Sunday of his life, September 17, 1967, when he went to his Father's home from the Lord's house.

It was natural that Sing-Hoh went to the Hinghwa Bible School to train for the minis-try. Our second term of service was in Hinghwa City where George was Principal of the Bible School, adding his love to teaching to that of preaching. He initiated a new course in which qualified students could take Middle School along with their Bible School courses, thus earning two diplomas Thus they were prepared for advanced studies in University and Seminary.

Sing-Hoh was one of the promising students who benefited from this deep concern for leadership development. He graduated from the B.A. Department of the Nanking Theological Seminary. Sing-Hoh himself loves to tell of how he was expecting to work with "Father" in school and evangelism on his return. And how bitterly disappointed he was when "Father" showed him a letter from the Hinghwa Church in Singapore asking for a minister, and urged him to accept this golden opportunity. Much against his own desires, he accepted and came to Singapore. So the long fruitful years in the Hinghwa Church, and the very sermons in this book are part of the gift George W. Hollister gave to the Church here.

After 13 years in Hinghwa, George Hollister returned to his Alma Mater, Ohio Wesleyan University. Here for 18 years he taught Bible to hundreds of students who still remember him and his teaching. Because of the need in postwar China for experienced workers and pleas of beloved Chinese colleagues, who returned to Hinghwa in 1946.We were thrilled with the open doors for evangelism; most of all, the large audiences of students from government and private schools. Most thrilling of all, the publishing of Christian tracts that were distributed all over China even after the Communists took over. A happy interlude was the Centennial of Methodism in China, and attending General Conference of1948 to which we were both elected as delegates from Malaysia, traveling to the General Conference in Boston, U.S.A.

After 5 years in Burma with visits to Malaysia with Bishop and Mrs. Archer and our dear Hang family, we were appointed to Seremban, Malaysia. Here, for almost three years, we were blessed with the love of the warm-hearted people of Wesley Church and the community. Of course, the Hang family in Singapore made it seem like home coming, and the chance to see some of the fruits of the ministry and Dr. Hollister had urged upon an unwilling migrant young preacher those years ago.

And now I know that my loved one is rejoicing that Benjamin Hang Heong-Hua, Hang Sing-Hoh's youngest son, is following in his Gong-gongs' and his father's foot-steps. Deng-Do, to preach the Gospel as his chief passion and soul's delight. He has a fine record of study and work at Garrett Theological Seminary where George Hollister received his B. Div. and was awarded his honorary Doctor of Divinity degree.

May God bless this book and the hearts that Hang Sing-Hoh's life and message may touch. That life is as truly a memorial to George Hollister as Hollister Chapel in Serem-ban Methodist School, Malaysia, the George Hollister R.E. Building and the beautifully jeweled memorial window in our Forest Chapel United Methodist Church where we spent eight happy years together. And where I continue to live in the little house with its garden he planted and loved. Though my heart, like his, belongs to the matchless fellow-ship that circles the earth, "Go ye into all the world and "Deng-Do", preach the Gospel.

Mrs. George W. Hollister
No. 1, Alcott Lane,
Greenhills, Cincinnati,
Ohio 45218
U.S.A.

MY CHRISTIAN TESTIMONY
PREFACE: BY DR. PAUL B. MEANS, PH. D.

Including eighty-five Christian Sermons, Religious Essays and ten Historical Essays on the Christian Church in the Far East – by Rev. Paul Sing-Hoh Hang.

It has been my privilege to have known Rev. Paul Sing-Hoh Hang and his family for over thirty years. When Mrs. Means and I first came to Singapore from Indonesia in 1929, Paul Hang was not only the pastor of the Hinghwa Methodist Church, but was also the Secretary of Chinese Christian Literature for the Chinese Churches. He was very closely associated with me in the work of the Methodist Book Room, at our offices, at No. 10, Mount Sophia Road, Singapore.

About the same time, the Southern Bell, the Chinese equivalent of the Methodist Malaysia Message, was inaugurated. From the beginning, Rev. Hang was on the Board of Editors and together with the Chief Editor, Rev. Andrew K.T. Chen, helped to develop this magazine as the leading Chinese Christian magazine for all the Chinese Churches of Singapore and Malaysia.

In his capacity, Rev. Hang had an important part in the training of pastors at the Annual Chinese Pastors' Institutes, for the work of the churches in Singapore, Malaysia and Borneo.

Paul was elected as the first Asian Ministerial delegate to the General Conference of the Methodist Church, held in Boston, U.S.A. in 1948.Besides his work in the Methodist Book Room, he was Secretary of Chinese Christian Literature and Education for eleven years from 1937 to 1948.For fifteen years, he was Editor of the Annual Conference minutes for the Malaysia Chinese Annual Conference (1938-1953), and also during this time he was Secretary of this Conference. He served as Associate Editor of the Southern Bell from 1928 to 1941 and from1947 to 1959.

All this time he was building up his Hinghwa congregation, at first on 27, Sam Leong Road, but later into the fine new Church, constructed shortly after World War II on Kitchener Road. Paul served as pastor of this church from the beginning of his ministry in Singapore until his retirement in 1963.He had served 36 years from 1927 to 1963.

Paul was born in Hinghwa, Fukien, China on May 3, 1901 to a Methodist family. His mother served as Bible woman in the Hinghwa Conference, China for twenty-one years.

On account of his ill health, Rev. Hang retired in 1963 but during these years of retirement, he has served as conference-evangelist and preacher in many of our Methodist churches in Malaysia, Singapore and Sarawak.

The following collection of eighty-five sermons, the Rev. Hang now presents to commemorate the 85th year (1985-1970) of the Methodist Church in Singapore and Malaysia; and to the memory of his parents, Mr. Hang Hu-Bu and Mrs. Hang Hu-Bu (Madam Deng Do-Di), and as a gift to the Church throughout the world.

As a second part of this book, Rev. Hang presents the history of the Chinese Methodist Church in Singapore and Malaysia, as he has known it so intimately all these many years.

It may be of interest to know that Rev. Hang received his theological training at Nanking Theological Seminary, China, with a B.A. in Theology in 1927.

He is the father of a large and closely-knit family of seven girls and six boys, eleven of whom are still living. Mrs. Hang has been a wonderful mother to all these children and is now the proud grandmother of twenty-four grandchildren, who are mostly in Singapore and Malaysia with some, however, living in Hong Kong and the U.S.A.

Six of his children have studied in various Methodist and other colleges in the U.S.A. In fact, his youngest, Benjamin, after having finished at Morningside College, Iowa, is now studying for the Methodist ministry in the Garrett Graduate

School of Theology, Evanston, Illinois. Benjamin has joined the Iowa Annual Conference of the United Methodist Church as an ordained deacon. Among Paul's sons-in-law are: Dr. Wong Kong Meng of Malacca, Dr. Robert Loh, an eye specialist of the General Hospital, Singapore, and Dr. Eddie Chan, Dental Surgeon in Hong Kong. Another son-in-law, Dr. Robert H. McKinley, Esther's husband, is an anthropologist at Michigan State University, in Ann Arbor, Michigan, U.S.A.

As Paul looks back over these rich past seventy years, he should hear in his heart the words, "Well done, good and faithful servant."

Dr. Paul B. Means   Mrs. Paul B. Means

Brief Biographical Notes:

Dr. Paul B. Means, a close family friend of Rev. Paul Hang, first came to Singapore as a Methodist missionary in 1929.During his many years of service to the local Christian community, he and his wife and family have gained the respect and esteem of many Christian families in Singapore and Malaysia.

In spite of advancing years, he and Mrs. Means continue to

work in various Christian Church and social activities for the furtherance of God's kingdom on earth. Their keen and selfless devotion to the Church, as a whole, and towards the welfare of all Asian peoples, in particular, bear testimony to their unique Christian character.

They have a lovely family of four grown-up children, Mariel, Gordon, Virginia and Charlotte, all of whom have achieved high academic success in Political Science, Architecture and Education.

Dr. Means received his B.A. degree from Yale University in 1915, B. Litt. From Oxford University in 1923 and Ph.D from Columbia University in 1935.From 1941 to 1959, he was Professor-Emeritus of Religion at the University of Oregon, U.S.A. while, at the same time, ministering to various Churches in Oregon. Although he has retired, he continues to serve a Church in Oregon, U.S.A.

Dr. & Mrs. Paul B. Means & Family

MY CHRISTIAN TESTIMONY
PREFACE BY: THE REV. S. T. PETER LIM

Saint Paul was forced into involuntary retirement by his arrest and imprisonment. But this did not silence his witness. Instead, he wrote letters to churches and individuals and these are embodied in the New Testament.

The Reverend Paul S. H. Hang has been forced into retirement by a combination of poor health and advancing years, but that has not meant the end of his ministry. He has continued to preach and to write The Southern Bell, an official publication of the Chinese Annual Conference of the Methodist Church in Singapore and Malaysia that carries regular contributions from him.

In his book, the Reverend Paul Hang has collected many of his sermons and other writings. These bear eloquent testimony to the quality of his preaching, his pastoral work, his spiritual life, his intimate knowledge of the Methodist Church and of other denominations in this area, and, above all, his stewardship as a servant of God.

The Reverend Paul Hang has served as the pastor of the Hinghwa Methodist Church for nearly forty years. He has been District Superintendent and Secretary of the Malaysia Chinese Annual Conference and its committees on Christian Literature and Religious Education among a host of other appointments, duties and responsibilities. In 1948 he was the first Asian delegate from Singapore and Malaya to attend the General

Conference of the Methodist Church in the United States of America. He was also Chairman of the Singapore Chinese Christian Church Union.

God has richly rewarded the Reverend Paul Hang for his dedication to His calling. He always places God above all, the Church next and himself last. His large family of sons and daughters have grown up and in their turn established God-fearing families.

His service is an inspiration and his life a hymn of praise to the Lord.

Brief Biographical Note:

The Rev. S. T. Peter Lim is the first secretary of the General Conference of the autonomous Methodist Church in Singapore and Malaysia. He played a leading role in the negotiation that led to the establishment of the new Church in 1968.

Among his many responsibilities to the Chinese Annual Conference, Mr. Lim is Chairman of the Boards of Finance and Missions and a member of the Executive Board. He is a lay delegate to the General Conference of the United Methodist Church, U.S.A. (1968, 1970 and 1972)

Mr. Lim serves on the Executive Board of the Council of Churches in Singapore and Malaysia and on the Board of Governors of the Trinity Theological College, Singapore.

He has served on various bodies such as the SCM, the YMCA. The Boy's Brigade and the Family Planning Association of the State of Negri Sembilan, Malaysia. He is currently Secretary of the Singapore National Kidney Foundation and the Singapore National Heart Association.

Mr. Lim works in the University of Singapore as the Public Relations Officer. Although he is designated PRO, his duties range from public relations to student affairs. Prior to his present appointment he was Principal of the Anglo-Chinese School of Seremban in Malaysia and a teacher and senior assistant in the Anglo-Chinese Secondary School in Singapore. He has lectured at the Singapore Teachers' Training College and the University of Malaya.

Educated at Raffles College, Singapore, the University of Malaya, Singapore; and the Union Theological Seminary, New York, he holds the degrees of B.A. Hons. and M.A. and the Diploma in Arts. He was awarded the PJK (Meritorious Service Medal) by the previous Ruler of the State of Negri Sembilan, Malaysia, in recognition of his public service. Mr. Lim is married and has a son, who is a lawyer and a daughter.

Mr. & Mrs. S. T. Peter Lim and their children

A BRIEF HISTORY OF THE HINGHWA METHODIST CHURCH, SINGAPORE
(BISHOP EDWIN F. LEE MEMORIAL)

By Rev. Paul S. H. Hang
Interpreted by: Rev. Tan Keat-Theang

In the year 1889, Rev. W. N. Brewster was appointed by the Board of Foreign Missions of the Methodist Episcopal Church in U.S.A. to be the Pastor of the Wesley Methodist Church, Singapore. At the end of 1890, he was transferred to Hinghwa, Fukien, China where he helped and extended churches, schools and hospitals.

Rev. Brewster had a first hand knowledge of the importance of Singapore being a great Trade Centre where traders from Europe and the West met people of the East. He knew that a great number of Hinghwa people had migrated to Singapore, among whom there were Methodist Christians. These Christians attended services at the Foochow Church,

Singapore but due to the dialect problem they were not too happy, and there was no progress in the work among the Hinghwa people.

So early in 1911, Rev. Brewster and Rev. Lee Tiong-Swee, on their way to Sibu, called at Singapore and visited the Hinghwa Church work. Seeing the dialect difficulty, they encouraged and helped to organize the Hinghwa Congregation. The Minutes of the Malaysia Conference held at Kuala Lumpur on 15th February,1912 has the following report by the District Superintendent Rev. W. T. Cherry:

"Chinese work has been done at five points, in four dialects: Hokkien, Foochow, Hakka and Hinghwa. An Epworth League has been organized to bring together the members of all five congregations. Hinghwa work was begun soon after Conference, but in October the preacher died of cholera. The work is being successfully supplied, but I hope to have a Hinghwa preacher soon. This church was formally organized two weeks ago with 8 probationers and 13 members.

The October 1911 Number of the Malaysia Message (Vol. 21, No. 11) on page 6, has the following:-

"Mr. Goh Bun-Lin, the recently appointed pastor of the Hinghwa Congregation in Singapore, was taken to the Quarantine Hospital on the 7th instant suffering from a severe attack of cholera...............Our latest advices report both patients in a dangerous condition. (Since writing the foregoing, both patients have died)"

After the death of Mr. Goh Bun-Lin, Mr. Tiu Cheng-Liong was appointed as supply pastor at the Malaysia Conference held on 15th February, 1912.

At the Malaysia Conference held on the 13th of February, 1913, the District Superintendent (Rev. A. J. Amery) reported as follows:-

"Hinghwa......We expected a regular preacher for this Congregation in October but such was not available, consequently Br. Tiu Cheng-Liong has given what care he could after attending the Anglo-Chinese School half the day and working as a clerk at the Press the other half – not an ideal arrangement."

In August 1913, the Rev. Deng Bing-Deng of the Hinghwa Conference was given the pastorate. As a result of good pastoral work of Rev. Deng Bing-Deng, the membership was greatly increased, and in 1916 there were 80 members. The Congregation worshipped in the Middle Road Church, but they also rented a shop house which they used for their prayer service and any other extra meetings. At this time, there were not many Hinghwa women attending the Church services.

Rev. Deng and his wife were very efficient and hard-working. Rev. Deng was also very methodical and seldom went to a meeting without a Discipline somewhere about his person, and he kept everyone, even the District Superintendent, in order.

In April 1919, due to serious physical ailment, Rev. Deng Bing-Deng was ordered to China by the doctor. During his absence, Mr. Tay Chaik-Gi was appointed to take charge He was assisted by Mr. James Huang. It was a great loss to the Church and his many friends when Mr. James Huang died in November, 1919.

Rev. Deng Bing-Deng was welcomed back from China in 1920. He resumed work as pastor of our church. In the winter of 1921 he had a relapse of his sickness and had to return to China, where he died on 8th July, 1923 at the early age of 42, being survived by his wife, 3 sons and 1 daughter. He death was an irreparable loss to the Hinghwa Congregation. He and Mrs. Deng during the period of his pastorage laid a firm foundation for the Hinghwa Church. Mrs. Deng especially worked very hard among the women of the Church.

Following the departure of the late Rev. Deng Bing-Deng at the end of 1921, Mr. H.B. Ling was appointed as supply pastor of our church. In April 1921, he was succeeded by Mr. Lau Hoe-Ching as pastor for about two years.

Then at the Malaysia Conference held on the 7th of January, 1924, the Rev. Yap It Tong was appointed as pastor. He served for 2 years and was succeeded by Mr. Chang Cheng-

Liang (a native of Foochow) in January, 1926. Due to the dialect difficulty, work of the Church was carried out by Messrs. H. B. Ling, Sie Teck-Hoe and Ling Kai-Cheng. For over a year there was no proper pastor. The Church wrote to Mr. Lau Lay-Cheong, the Principal of the Guthrie Memorial High School, Putien City, Fukien Province, China to look for a good pastor from Hinghwa.

In June, 1927, Mr. Lau replied, recommending Mr. Paul Sing-Hoh Hang, a B.A. Course graduate of the Nanking Theological Seminary, to be pastor of the Church. The District Superintendent (Dr. Edwin F. Lee) and our Church accepted the recommendation of Mr. Lau and Mr. Hang arrived with his wife (Madam Ng So-Ging) on 4th August, 1927. A welcoming function was given on the 25th of August at the Tamil Methodist Church in Short Street. Mr. Hang's appointment started from July 1927 the day he left Fukien, China.

During the past 34 years, since his appointment, Rev. Paul S. H. Hang, with great love for God and the Hinghwa Church, has faithfully and with great zeal, served the Church. In spite of great difficulty, with God's help and the co-operation of members of the Church, work among the Hinghwa people has advanced steadily, and in addition a large and beautiful Church, with parsonage and Church Hall, has been successfully completed at a cost of approximately $150.000/-

Madam Tay Siok-Chin was the first person to be appointed as Women Preacher of our Church, in 1919. Prior to this no appointment was made, as there were very few women members in the Congregation. Madam Tay visited Sibu in 1920. During her absence of 6 months, Madam Nay Bok-Tee acted in her place. On her return from Sibu, she resumed work. She served until the end of 1929, when, owing to ill-health due to her faithful and hard work, she had to retire and live with her people in Sibu, Sarawak.

Madam Aw Ah-Soon succeeded Madam Tay, and she served from 1930 until 1932. Following this there was no woman preacher until 1936 when Madam Lim Leong-Go came on transfer from the Malacca Church. She left at the end of 1937.

In the fall of 1935, the great Evangelist Dr. John Sung visited Singapore and Malaya from China. As a result of his great inspiring revival meeting, never before experienced, the Singapore Evangelist Bank was organized. The Hinghwa Church Evangelistic Band was affiliated to this Band. Misses Yeo Siok-Ching and Ong Geok-Ting were elected president and vice-president, respectively, of our Evangelistic Band. Under their able leadership, evangelistic work has been carried on unceasingly for 26 years up to the present time. Since 1937, no Bible woman has been appointed as the work was faithfully and successfully carried out by the members of the Evangelistic Band. An able Christian worker, Miss Toan Kheng Hua was the pianist at the old church at Sam Leong Road for 7 years. From August, 1956, the Malaysia Chinese Annual Conference appointed Mrs. Tai Ah Loi as a volunteer worker in Women's Work.

The Methodist Church has always been interested in the work of the Hinghwa Church. It has not only contributed large sums of money to help complete the new Church but also appointed missionaries to help us in the work of the Church. The following are some of the Missionaries who have served in our Church:

(1) Miss D. Olson   (2) Miss Hammond   (3) Miss White
(4) Miss Jackson   (5) Mrs. Miner   (6) Rev. J. F. Peat
(7) Miss Ruth Harvey (8) Miss Birdice Lawrence
(9) Rev. H. L. Sone   (10) Miss Ellen H. Suffern

Of these Missionaries, Miss Suffern was the only one who could speak the Hinghwa dialect and she served the longest in our Church (8 years.). We are very grateful to all these Missionaries for their help and guidance to our Church.

In 1948, when Rev. Paul S. H. Hang was elected as Ministerial Delegate to the General Conference at Boston, U.S.A., Bishop Edwin F. Lee and the District Superintendent

Rev. Hong Han Keng appointed Mr. Sie Teck-Hoe to be Honorary Associate Pastor of the Hinghwa Church and to be in charge of our Church during the absence of Rev. Paul S. H. Hang. In addition, Mr. Sie was been a keen worker in the Sunday School for many years, having been Superintendent at various times and having been responsible and conscientious in the Sunday School program.

For over ten years, Mr. Kao Chin-Jen was the choir director having contributed immensely to the music program of the Church. Since 1948, his wife, Mrs. Kao Tai Ching-Ying, was keenly interested in the Hinghwa-speaking M.Y.F. and was instrumental in forming the local M.Y.F. in 1950. Under her able leadership, the M.Y.F. was a success. She also enlisted her help in the local Sunday School and the Women's Society of Christian Service.

In October 1959, Rev. Paul S. H. Hang, who was approaching 60 years of age, and due to the increasing work of the Church, thought that he should have someone to help him. He accordingly invited Mr. Yeo Ming-Hong to work with him. In August 1960, the Annual Conference officially appointed him as Associate Pastor of our Church. Rev. Tan Keat-Theang was also appointed to our Church in an Honorary capacity for one year.

For over 20 years from the beginning, the Hinghwa Congregation had no church building or parsonage of their own. They moved from one place to another. First they rented a place in Serangoon Road, then they moved to Middle Road and thence to Short Street. This constant move was not only a shame to our congregation but also did not glorify the Name of God. This matter was a constant concern of the pastor. So in 1933, a Quarterly Conference was convened and a Building Committee was formed.

With the help of the District Superintendent, Rev. Abel Eklund, a grant of $4,000/- was given to our Church from the sale of the Middle Road Church property. Over $2,000/- was also raised from members and friends. A shop house (No. 27

Sam Leong Road) and furniture were bought at the cost of $6,200/- and, for the first time, the Hinghwa Congregation had a Church of their own. The ground floor was converted to be used for a place of worship and the pastor and his family lived on the first floor.

The Church and parsonage were dedicated by the Bishop Edwin F. Lee at 3:00 p.m. on September 3, 1933. At the same service of Dedication, the Rev. Paul S. H. Hang was ordained an Elder of the Methodist Church.

By the end o f 1935, after the revival meetings conducted by the great Evangelist Dr. John Sung, the church premises became too small for the large number of members. Plans were then made to build a new church with seating accommodation for 1,000 members.

Dr. R. L. Archer helped us to purchase the present site of our church in Kitchener Road, measuring 7400 square feet, at $8,200/- in 1941. Due to the occupation of Singapore by the Japanese, our plans to build a new church had to be postponed.

In 1948, after attending the General Conference, Rev. Hang campaigned for funds for our new church building in the States. He was straightaway promised U.S. $5,000/- from the Advance Special by Bishop Lee, Dr. Archer and Dr. Dodsworth.

On our Pastor's return, steps were taken for the early erection of our church. Plans were drawn up by Mr. Chan Kui Chuan. Tenders were called and Mr. Ng Leong-Joo was accepted as the contractor.

On November 6, 1949, the cornerstone was laid by the Mission Superintendent, the Rev. Dr. M. Dodsworth, and the church building was completed in February, 1950, in time to be dedicated by Bishops Arthur J. Moore, Clement D. Rockey and R.L. Archer when the first Southeastern Asia Central Conference was in session. The Church was dedicated on February 6, 1950. Both these ceremonies were overwhelmingly and unprecedentedly attended by more than a thousand members and friends.

The whole project cost a total of $150,000/-. The new church was built in a combined Eastern and Western style. It consists of the church, church hall and the parsonage. It has a stately external appearance with Chinese style of roof, and a beautiful interior, with seating accommodation for 800.

The church was dedicated in memory of the late Bishop Edwin F. Lee for his long dedicated service in Malaya and the special attention and care he paid to the Hinghwa Church. It was named: "The Hinghwa Methodist church (Bishop Edwin F. Lee Memorial)".

All the members of the congregation were very happy with the completion of the new church. However, after sometime they felt that the sanctuary was not large enough. So in 1955, the piece of land at the back of the church, measuring 1200 square feet, was bought for $2,000/-. In 1956, the late Miss Ruth Lim donated $10,000/- to the church for the extension of the church in memory of her loving parents. The extension includes the sanctuary and office on the ground floor to the left of the Sanctuary and a first floor above the office used as an Upper Room. The extension came to a cost of over $40,000/-.

What our Church is today, and what had been accomplished during these 50 years, have been through the grace of God, and the interest shown by the faithful servants of the past and the faithfulness of all present members of our Church and friends.

May we, therefore, be thankful to our Heavenly Father, and look forward with ever increasing hope to the improvement of the Church. Let us hope and endeavor, with the help of God, to bring more people to Him. May we do all things to the glory of God, and may He grant His blessings upon us all.

(Extract from the 50th Anniversary Souvenir
of the Hinghwa Methodist Church)
Dated: April 20, 1962.

A great historical event took place on April 31, 1961, when the Hinghwa Methodist Church celebrated its Golden 50th Anniversary. To mark the occasion, a Thanksgiving Service was held at 4:00 p.m. on that memorable day with the Rev. Paul S. H. Hang as the Chairman and Bishop H. B. Amstutz as guest preacher and Miss Rebecca Deh-Hua Hang at the organ. It was truly an occasion to remember and which climaxed with a 20-table sumptuous dinner to celebrate the occasion.

The historic event was commemorated with the printing of the Hinghwa Methodist Church 50th Anniversary Souvenir which was edited by the Rev. Paul S. H. Hang, as editor-in-chief. The Souvenir received wide circulation among all the church members as well as other churches. This 200-page Souvenir, containing numerous photographic records of the Church's history and messages of greetings, cost $3,897/-

Immediately following this, Rev. Paul S. H. Hang was forced by ill-health to retire from active ministry in this Church in August, 1963.Due to a heart condition and gallstone ailment, Rev. Hang was advised by medical sources to retrain from active church work. Meanwhile, the Church Official Board organized a thanksgiving and farewell service to honor Rev. Hang's 36 years' dedicated service to the Hinghwa Methodist Church. At the same time, Rev. Hang was appointed Advisor to the Church.

The need to fill the vacancy created by Rev. Hang's retirement was fulfilled with the appointment of the Rev. Daniel Yu Li-Ching as the new pastor on December 1, 1963, with the recommendation of Rev. Paul S. H. Hang. Not long afterwards, the Mandarin-speaking Service was organized.

With the arrival of the Rev. James T. S. Ling, after retirement from the Sarawak Annual Conference in 19968, the Church invited him to be their Honorary Pastor. In this capacity, Rev. Ling and 2 retired pastors frequently assisted in the Communion Services – a unique scene seldom seen in the Methodist Church in Singapore and Malaysia.

During the last 7 years' of retirement, Rev. Paul S. H. Hang continued to service the Hinghwa Methodist Church on voluntary basis, with frequent invitations to preach in this Church as well as other local churches in Singapore and Malaysia. Now in his 70th year, he and Mrs. Hang continue to serve God and His Church in their own quiet way. By the grace of God, occasioned by his retirement, Rev. Paul S. H. Hang found the opportunity to write his Book of Sermons and his Christian Testimony, to the Glory of God.

By the grace and bounteous blessings of God, the Hinghwa Methodist Church has now grown to a full membership of 340, with 576 preparatory members, making a total membership of 916, comprising 174 families. May the Almighty God continue to nurture the wonderful growth of this Church both spiritually and physically, in the years ahead.

By: Rev. Tan Keat-Theang
Dated: June 25, 1970.

Rev. and Mrs. Tan Keat-Theang

EXTENDING THE KINGDOM
OF GOD TODAY

Scripture Lesson: Isaiah 54: 1-3

Scripture Text: Isaiah 54:2

"For you will spread abroad to the right and to the left, and your descendents will possess the nations and will people the desolate cities."

In the ancient times, the people of Israel lived mostly in tents. They even made use of these tents as sanctuaries unto God. As the years passed, the number of persons increased and they were faced with the necessity of building bigger and stronger tents. This is representative of the growth of the number of Christians and the number of Christ's Churches today.

Our Lord promised the descendents of the Israelites that they would possess many nations and that they would also inhabit the desolate cities. Our Lord laid down the condition that they should spread abroad to the right and to the left. They needed to enlarge their dwelling-tents, to lengthen their cords, and also to strengthen their stakes. In the spiritual sense, our Lord in the same way would like each one of us to extend His kingdom regardless of time and place.

He would like to see that we proclaim the Good News to

peoples of different races. In the Lord's Prayer, we pray, "Thy kingdom come, thy will be done on earth as it is in heaven." Christians believe that the Kingdom of God is here and now and that it is implanted in the souls of all Christians. We Christians need to go out and proclaim the Gospel not only with our words but also with our deeds.

Before His Ascension, Jesus commanded his disciples to be His witnesses in Jerusalem and in all Judea and Samaria and to the end of the earth. The big cities of Singapore and Kuala Lumpur are representative of our Judea. The new villages in Malaysia are representative of Samaria and also the end of the earth. It is my sincere hope that every Christian in this area will reach out to another non-Christian friend and bring him to Christ.

"But how do we extend God's Kingdom?" you may ask. Firstly, we need to have an unreserved love for God and for our fellow men. Our Lord said, "Enlarge the place of your tent, and lengthen our cords." This word "cords" may be interpreted as our unreserved love for God and our fellow men. Unless we possess this, our preaching and witnessing will come to naught. We should never be content with the work that we have achieved. But rather, we need constantly to remind ourselves of God's call to service and obedience. Hosea 11:4 says, "When Israel was a child, I loved him, and out of Egypt I called my son. I led them with cords of compassion, with the bonds of love and I became to them as one who eases the yoke on their jaws, and I bent down to them and fed them." Our love for God and our fellow men must have depth, width and length, just like God's love for us.

Secondly, we need to pray earnestly for the work of the Methodist Church in this area and also for one another. Our Lord commanded us to strengthen our stakes. What are our stakes and how are they to be interpreted? Literally, stakes are used to keep tents firm and in position. At the same time, they are buried deep in the ground and cannot be seen. The "stakes" may be interpreted as the earnest prayer that we offer for the work of our individual churches and also for our fellow workers and members. These prayers may be held in homes, in churches, or in public buildings.

The world's famous evangelists, such as Dr. Spurgeon, Dr. Billy Graham and many others, achieved their successes in public meetings through the unceasing prayers of Christians throughout the world. So it was with the success of Dr. John Sung, the great evangelist. Today, Christians need to pray without ceasing for the mission work of the Church and also for the salvation of thousands of lost souls in the world. We should never allow Satan to be a big obstacle in the midst of our preaching and witnessing. St. Paul, the great apostle and saint, urged his fellow Christians to pray earnestly to his work. The urgency is laid upon us to pray for the church and at the same time to witness to the grace and love of our Lord Jesus Christ. St. Paul, in one of his Epistles said, "Woe unto me, if I preach not the Gospel."

The Methodist Church in Asia and the South Pacific has a history of 85 years. In February 1885, missionary work was first started in Singapore by Bishops Thoburn and Oldham who came from South India. They began to proclaim the love of God to the natives there. In 1892, the work spread to Malaya. In 1899, mission work was started n the Philippines. In 1901, missionary work began in Sarawak, and then spread to Sumatra and Java, Indonesia in 1905.

Seventeen years later in 1902, from 21st February to 27th February, the first Annual Conference was established in Singapore. It was known as the first session of the Malaysia Mission Conference of the Methodist Church.

In August, 1927, God called me to serve as a pastor of the Hinghwa Methodist Church, Singapore. I served in that church for thirty-six years and retired in 1964. During the past forty-two years, I saw very clearly for myself the rapid growth of the Methodist Church in Malaysia and Singapore. In 1948, the Malaysia Chinese Annual Conference was organized. At this Conference, it was reported that there were 61 churches, 24

Chapels, 8074 preparatory members, 7115 full members, 2 High Schools, 3 Primary Schools and 4 Kindergarten. In 1952, the Sarawak Annual Conference was organized. It was reported that there were 55 Churches, 26 Chapels, 15,308 preparatory members, 4,944 adult baptisms, 19,838 full members, 6 High Schools, 5 Integrated Primary Schools and 7 Kindergartens.

In February, 1962, the Iban Provisional Conference was organized. It was reported that there were 8 Churches, 143 Chapels, 4,043 preparatory members, and 7,905 members. The Malaya Annual Conference was organized in 1902. It was reported that there were 62 churches, 3,766 preparatory members, 13,200 members,66 Primary & Secondary Schools, 16 Girls' Schools, and 14 Kindergartens. In December, 1968, the Tamil Provisional Conference was brought into existence.

In February, 1950, I was privileged to attend the first session of the Southeastern Asia Central Conference. During the closing session of this same Conference in August, 1968, I was called upon to say the closing prayer. This gave way to the establishment of the Constituting Conference of the Methodist Church in Malaysia and Singapore. During the opening session, I was called upon to address the delegates who were representing the Malaya Annual Conference, the Malaysia Chinese Annual Conference, the Sarawak Annual Conference and the Iban Provisional Conference.

With God's blessing and the guidance given by the General Conference of the Methodist Church (U.S.A.) and also the work put forth by the past church workers, the Methodist Church in this area brought forth many fruits of their concern and hard labor. It is our duty to preserve this good work and continue to strive to win more souls for Christ.

It is my sincere hope that in the near future these existing Conferences will become Jurisdictional Conferences. And in turn they will form a Great General Conference. This will only be realized through our sincere love for God and our fellow men and by remembering always to pray without ceasing for the work of the Church and also for the lost souls.

Now that the new Methodist Church in Malaysia and Singapore has been established, I beseech you to seek the guidance of the Holy Spirit in our work, to put forth our energy towards our work, also to put forth our faith, hope and love. Let us always remember to put God first in our lives and our work, and at the same time to sacrifice ourselves in this cause in love and prayer, ever seeking to extend the Kingdom of God in Malaysia and Singapore. Unto Him be honor and praise and unto us His abundant blessings. Amen.

Sermon delivered by: REV. PAUL S. H. HANG
Interpreted by: JOHN D. H. HANG
Dated: October, 1968

HINGHWA METHODIST CHURCH, SINGAPORE

MAJOR PAST EVENTS

Leaders at the Hinghwa Methodist Church's 60th Birthday

Hinghwa Methodist Church

一九四九年佈道隊影

Evangelistic Band at 27, Sam Leong Road Church in 1949

六十週年紀念聖歌團影

Pastors & the Hinghwa Methodist Church Choir - 1961

一九六一年慶祝

60th Anniversary Thanksgiving Service & Celebration

新嘉坡興化音天道堂

五十二歲時之范新福牧

Rev. Paul S. H. Hang, Sr.

The "bicycle" Pastor

IMAGES FROM THE PAST

The Hinghwa Methodist Church – newly built in 1950

Evangelistic Band at Sam Leong Road - 1939

Senior members of the Hinghwa Methodist Church

Chin Lien Bible Institute represented at the 60th
Anniversary Service

一九三九年佈道隊影　　一九六一年鄰女服務會職員影　　一九六一年佈道隊影

新嘉坡興化音天道堂

范新福諤道集

一八二

新范，師牧庭戀黃
督會伯和安，師牧福

Rev. Hang & Dr. Dodsworth

Rev. Hang, Bishop Amstutz, Rev. Huang

IN PERSPECTIVE

Church members bid farewell to Rebecca & Paul Hang Jr.

Church leaders and board members in 1953

Rev. Paul S. H. Hang preaching at the 60th Anniversary Service

Rev. Paul Hang's father visited Singapore - 1937

Author Paul Hang Jr's family with his parents - 1970

ABOUT THE AUTHOR

The author, Paul K.H. Hang Jr. is one of the twelve children in the "Hang" family of Singapore with the nickname, "Cheaper by the Dozen" all of whom were born in Singapore. He is the 2nd son and the 5th child of the late Rev. and Mrs. Paul S.H. Hang Sr. who emigrated from Sienyu, Fukien Province, mainland China in 1927 to  serve the Hinghwa Methodist Church in Singapore and to preach the gospel to the nations.

A citizen of the United States of America, Paul Jr. is now retired and resides in Ohio, U.S.A. With a keen interest in reading and world affairs, he finds pleasure in intellectual interacting with people and he loves to share his life's experiences and testimonies. He was born on April 3, 1932 and he received his primary and secondary education at the Anglo-Chinese School, Singapore where he graduated in 1952. He obtained his B.Sc. degree from Oregon State College in Corvallis, Oregon in 1957. He had over 25 years' engineering career working with multi-national companies in San Francisco, Singapore. and Malaysia from 1957 to 1983. Before his retirement, he worked for 5 years' with McMillan Publishing Inc. in Chicago. He is blessed with a wealth of experience having lived over 30 years in Asia and another 30 years in the U.S.A.

At an early age of 4 years old, Paul Jr. came close to losing his life when he was stricken with high fever at the time when many young children died of such illnesses as cholera, dysentery and even high fever. By the grace and mercy of God, his life was spared by an act of kindness of a missionary couple, Rev. & Mrs. G. Summers who used ice to save his life!

When Paul Jr. was born, his parents gave him his Chinese name "Kee-Hua" which represents the country of Italy in Chinese. His parents thought of a unique way of naming their 12 children by using the names of 12 countries and translating them into Chinese. Thus he was given the name "Kee" or Italy and "Hua", the Chinese word to indicate his Chinese ethnicity. He was baptized later and given the biblical name Paul Jr., thus his full name became Paul Kee-Hua Hang, Jr.

Coming from a poor and needy preacher's family, Paul Jr. was miraculously blessed with good financial support from a Christian philanthropist to study in America. His American degree in civil engineering was his passport to a whole new world of engineering opportunities. His engineering career encompassed many aspects of civil engineering, marine engineering and the petroleum industry. He has worked in San Francisco, Singapore as well as Malaysia.

Paul Jr. now lives with his wife Doris in Streetsboro, Ohio where he is a free-lance writer and a happy grandfather. He enjoys traveling to Asia, specifically Singapore, where he had his roots. He is blessed with good health and he enjoys frequent visits to his children and grandchildren in Brunswick, Ohio, Lisle, Schaumburg, Illinois and Groton, Connecticut. His strong desire is to serve God and help improve the livelihood of his fellow Chinese, particularly the Chinese Christians in mainland China. He loves to read and share his experiences and testimonies, to glorify God and to honor his parents who devoted their lives to serving God and His Church and to "preach the gospel to the nations".

A Final Word….. A Tribute….

IN MEMORIAM

"They shall not grow old
As we that are left grow old
Age shall not weary them
Nor years condemn.
At the going down of the sun
And in the morning
We shall remember them…"

We give thanks to the Lord for the lives of……..

Our Beloved Parents

Rev. Paul Sing-Hoh Hang, Sr.   Mrs. Paul S. H. Hang, Sr. (Ng So-Ging)
(1901 – 1972)   *(1901 – 1975)*

Our Beloved Brothers

Peter Hang Gong-Hua   John Hang Diong-Hua   David Hang Hing-Hua
(1929 – 1961)   *(1936 – 1982)*   *(1941 – 1997)*

Rev. Benjamin Hang Heong-Hua
(1943 – 1986)

Our Beloved Sister

Mrs. Wong Kong Meng (Rebecca Hang Deh-Hua)
(1931 – 1999)

May the words of Psalm 23 on the following page be of comfort and peace to all their loved ones and friends. May He be your Shepherd and your guiding Light always.

The Lord is my shepherd; I shall not want.

He maketh me to lie down in green pastures; He leadeth me beside the still waters.

He restoreth my soul; He leadeth me in the paths of righteousness for His name's sake.

Yea, though I walk through the valley of the shadow of death, I will fear no evil: for thou art with me; thy rod and thy staff they comfort me.

Thou preparest a table before me in the presence of mine enemies: thou annointest my head with oil; my cup runneth over.

Surely goodness and mercy will follow me all the days of my life and I will dwell in the house of the Lord for ever.

Psalm 23.

Original Artwork by:
Faul Kee-Hua Hang Jr.
A.C.S. Class of 1951

Printed in the United States
47523LVS00001B/1-90